The
ROCK BOTTOM
PARADOX

The
ROCK BOTTOM
PARADOX

A blueprint for turning adversity
into opportunity

NICHOLAS WALLWORK
AND
MARTIN FOSTER

First published in Great Britain in 2025

Copyright © Nicholas Wallwork and Martin Foster

The moral right of the author has been asserted.

All rights reserved.

No part of this publication may be reproduced, stored in a retrieval system, or transmitted, in any form or by any means, without the prior permission in writing of the publisher, nor be otherwise circulated in any form of binding or cover other than that in which it is published and without a similar condition including this condition being imposed on the subsequent purchaser.

Published by Quartz Press.
quartzpress.com

ISBN: 978-1-917329-50-7

Contents

A Message from Nicholas	iii
A Message from Martin	v
Authors' Acknowledgements	vii
Connect With Us	x

Introduction — 1

Part I: The Bottom — 9

Chapter 1 FACING YOUR LOSS (WHATEVER IT MAY BE) — 11

Chapter 2 BECOMING YOUR OWN PRIORITY — 26

Chapter 3 FINDING GRATITUDE AND POSITIVITY (EVEN WHEN LIFE KNOCKS YOU BACK) — 47

Chapter 4 FREEING YOURSELF THROUGH FORGIVENESS — 62

Part II: Preparing For The Climb — 79

Chapter 5 FINDING YOUR WHY — 81

Chapter 6 SETTING YOUR GOALS (BIG AND SMALL) — 95

Chapter 7 **CREATING A ROUTINE THAT SUPPORTS YOUR JOURNEY**   111

Chapter 8 **OVERCOMING FEAR AND TAKING THE FIRST STEP**   124

Part III: The Climb Itself   141

Chapter 9 **STAYING FOCUSED ON ONE STEP AT A TIME**   143

Chapter 10 **HARNESSING THE POWER OF MINDSET**   153

Chapter 11 **STAYING MOTIVATED (HINT: IT'S ABOUT PEOPLE)**   174

Chapter 12 **HELPING OTHERS ALONG THE WAY**   189

Part IV: The Journey

Chapter 13 **WHY LIVING IS THE JOURNEY**   203

What To Read Next   215

Connect With Us   216

A Message From Nicholas

Nicholas Wallwork is a multi-millionaire property investor, developer, International For Dummies author, and accredited property educator and mentor. Well-known for his role on SKY TV and Amazon Prime as a property investment angel on both "Property Elevator" and "Property Mentors", Nicholas has a highly respected name within the property sector and regularly appears as a property market commentator on TV, YouTube, podcasts, radio and at national property events.

Nicholas fell into property in 2002 when he realised turning his first house into a small HMO (rather than living in it himself) made complete financial sense. HMOs and commercial-to-residential development were to form key strategies of his successful property career. Aged just 25 he had no mortgage or bills to pay and could effectively retire (albeit modestly), teaching him a very early lesson that passive income from assets (property and investments) was the way to build long-term wealth and a flexible, comfortable and happy lifestyle.

Today, Nicholas has developed in excess of £100 million worth of UK property and owns a group of successful property businesses, including a property development consultancy, a business consultancy, several development companies and a lettings and management business. Just like the Extraordinary Millionaire sister book, the authors believe that for wealth to be truly sustainable it needs to encompass and permeate all areas of life. True wealth starts in the mind. It crystalises purpose and passion, it becomes a way of life, it enables freedom, it encourages compassion, and it ensures legacy.

However! Any journey through life is never plain sailing and Nicholas definitely faced his share of "Rock Bottoms". Surviving the credit crunch, Covid, hyperinflationary periods, dramatic market shifts as well as personal loss were some of the biggest, teaching him many important lessons which he shares with you through this book and indeed through The Extraordinary Millionaire book series and associated coaching and consultancy businesses. "To be successful in life or any business you need to stay at the top of your game" - This means continually educating yourself and improving your skills and knowledge to further your business and personal success. But before you can do this, you need to be able to use the same skills to pull you out of your "Rock Bottom"! I'm very passionate about helping others with the lessons I've learned. I've only had some success today because I used these tools to get through the most challenging times in my life... I've been downright depressed at times in my life, and it doesn't matter where you are in life (success or money-wise) the feelings of depression can be the same. Mental health isn't a taboo subject anymore and I hope this book helps you talk about it and most importantly provides some of the tools that can help *you* move to a better place.

SHARING SOME DEDICATED GRATITUDE

This book is dedicated to my soul mate and amazing wife, Britta Wallwork, and to my amazing, always positive family Siènna, Skyla, and Silàs. Thank you, Britta, for believing in me always and without question, right from the outset, especially when I was feeling down. I'm lucky to have the best team mate help me through some of my dark hours and for that I'm truly grateful.

A Message from Martin

I would love to say that I started writing this book with you the reader in mind. That I started with some grand intention to better the world, to help others, to share some profound knowledge, to change lives, to teach and to guide. The truth is I can't. You see this book started at a time when I was at my very own Rock Bottom.

The life that I had taken for granted for so long, had come crashing down around me. It was sudden, it was abrupt, it was unexpected and if I am honest, I was devastated. I know what it is like to experience despair, anger, fear, and sadness. I understand the range of emotions that a person goes through at Rock Bottom. Most of all I understand how difficult it is to see Rock Bottom as an opportunity, especially when you're in that dark place, because that is exactly where I was.

I also know that often opportunity will appear exactly when you need it most. For me it was by way of my co-author Nicholas. We had often spoken of writing something together, but the stars had yet to align. Yet as we spoke, we realised that both of us in our own way was experiencing our own version of Rock Bottom. More importantly, we realised that almost subconsciously we were both using similar tools for support and to work our way through. It was from this place that The Rock Bottom Paradox was born.

You see, for me this book was written for a very selfish reason, it was a form of catharsis, a way of picking myself up from my Rock Bottom. It was my Blueprint for turning adversity into opportunity. Why am I telling you this? Because I want you to know that the Blueprint has been tested, and that it works. I want you to know that someone else does understand what you are going through, has been through it, and has come out the other side. Most of all I want to let you know that it's all okay, how you are feeling is normal, and that no matter how difficult it all feels now, it will get better.

MARTINS' DEDICATION

This book is dedicated to my four children, Emily, Ben, Jude, and Cameron. The four of you remind me every day of how much I have, to be grateful for, have shown me what strength really is and above all else you are what I am most proud of.

Authors' Acknowledgements

NICHOLAS WOULD LIKE TO THANK...

A big thank you to my whole team for helping us deliver our unique development projects and for helping change the face of wealth creation and personal development forever. I'd also like to thank our extended project management team and trusted "power team" consultants who we work with across our various companies, without whom we would not be able to produce the results for our mentees & consultation clients that we do.

A huge thanks to Martin Foster my co-author. Writing this book was unique timing for both of us going through one if not the hardest years of our lives for different reasons. I'm sure people think we make it look easy sometimes, writing books, starting businesses, putting ourselves out there on TV, YouTube and social media, helping others and building multiple people's wealth... I can assure you behind the scenes we also have major challenges to overcome and lots of stress to deal with and "The Rock Bottom Paradox" was the perfect time to share how our much relied on mindset tools come to good use not only when you're at the top of your game but *even more importantly* when you're at your own Rock Bottom and need that help the most.

On a personal note, I'd like to send my deep gratitude and heartfelt thanks to Salarah who has been my own life coach for over a decade now. She has help me hone my own mindset when I needed it most. She's re-aligned me notably on two occasions (one of which was the year

I wrote this book) when I had run out of my own tools in my toolkit and she's a powerhouse of mindset & law of attraction knowledge and insanely talented life coach. Whether I've been looking to fine tune myself at peak performance or help me get out of a rut when I've hit a period of Rock Bottom, when I've turned to her for guidance, she has always inspired me and helped me level up to the next level. She's taught me to ask "Why is this happening *for* me?" Not "to me".

Thank you to all my investors, Joint Venture partners, mentees and consultation clients for your support and engagement as you all embark on your own wealth creation journeys. I'm grateful to have been able to help so many people achieve so much and seeing you do well is one of my biggest goals in life. Onwards and Upwards!

Finally, I want to thank my Mum and my late Father. The year I wrote this book my Dad passed away and a couple of months after that my Mum nearly died from a perforated bowl operation (that's how my Dad actually died two months earlier). Mum was in a coma for what seemed like an eternity after her operation and for a while we thought we might be in a position where we'd have to "switch off the machine". I can't begin to tell you how hard those days and weeks were by her bedside willing her to recover. This was all happening when we had just moved to another country (Holland my wife's native country) which without knowing was the worse timing ever and I felt I was abandoning her. On the business front, interest rates were shooting through the roof, properties weren't selling, and the market conditions were terrible. It is only when you get older you start to really appreciate why your parents are who they are. They had their own struggles in life just like we have, and they were born in a less forgiving time in many ways. Given time, I now have come to love, respect and forgive them for who they are/were and for all the good and the bad traits they possess(ed) which in one way or another have helped to shape me.

This was clearly for me one of the hardest years of my life bar none and that's why I'm grateful for this this book as it was an opportunity to share my journey and personal use of the mindset tools I knew and re-connected with and to put them to good effect in a different setting. Wherever you are in your own life these tools we're shared with you in *Rock Bottom* will help you level up and survive your darkest days just like I have.

MARTIN WOULD LIKE TO THANK...

First and foremost, a big thank you to my fellow founder Nicholas. You have become more than a colleague and mentor; you have become a friend and confidant.

To my friends and family who have always gone above and beyond for me, and without whom my journey from rock bottom would have been so much harder. It is truly humbling to have people in your life who will do so much without an expectation of anything in return. So, Thank You, Thank You, Thank You.

I would also like to thank my counsellor (she knows who she is). I will be forever grateful that I found a great counsellor in her.

My final thank you and acknowledgement goes to my father and best friend. Even though you are no longer with us, you remind me every day what it means to be a man, and a father. It's crazy that the lessons that you taught me so long ago are the ones that I'm only just beginning to understand now.

Connect With Us

As you work your way through this book, you may find that you have questions regarding some of the protocols we discuss. You may find yourself unsure of how to implement some of the steps into your daily routine. Or you may just want to reach out for support or to support others going through the same thing. At these times please reach out to us.

We would also love to hear what you think about the book. Which chapters resonated with you? Which bits made you sit up and say 'Yes! I've been there!' Which parts made the most difference on your own journey from rock bottom?

You can connect with Nicholas on Instagram (@nicholas_wallwork), on LinkedIn or via nicholaswallwork.com

You can connect with Martin via www.linkedin.com/in/martinfosterwealth or through our website www.extraordinarymillioniare.com (incidentally, this is also where you can find details about the other books, classes, coaching and mentorship programmes in the Extraordinary Millionaire Series).

We can't wait to hear from you!

ALSO BY NICHOLAS WALLWORK

The Extraordinary Millionaire

Professional Property Strategies

Advanced Property Development

Investing In International Real Estate **For Dummies**

Real Estate Investing (All-In-One) **For Dummies**

The Property Mentors

Introduction

LET'S TALK ABOUT ROCK BOTTOM

Rock bottom is universal, but also totally unique.

Most of us will hit rock bottom at some point in our life. That point when it all seems hopeless, like everything that you have worked for is gone, and everything you dreamed of has evaporated. You might feel like a failure. You may feel angry or even guilty. You might feel like no one else could possibly understand what it's like to be at rock bottom. When the truth is, you're not alone. Rock bottom happens to many people. It's certainly happened to us.

And yet rock bottom is so uniquely personal. Everyone's rock bottom is different.

Rock bottom can be sudden, like the death of a loved one, or a relationship breaking down, or being made redundant. But it can also be a slow buildup of circumstances over a long period of time, like worsening mental health, or getting into debt over a period of years.

Rock bottom can be financial. It can be emotional. It can be a career low. It can also be that awkward period when one phase of life ends and you're simply not sure what comes next. In this way, leaving university and trying to find your way as an adult might feel like a form of rock bottom. Retiring from a long and happy career might feel like a form of rock bottom. Your children leaving home. Becoming a carer for a loved one.

And of course, you might have some parts of your life going well while others are in the toilet. Maybe you're succeeding at work but coping with grief or divorce. Maybe you're going through a major health issue but are surrounded by a loving family.

In other words, you don't need to be in a heap, crying on the bathroom floor to read this book. You might need to overcome challenges in one specific part of life. You might simply be leaving one phase of life behind and unsure of the path ahead.

Life has seasons. Sometimes it feels like a gorgeous summer day, when you have the sea breeze in your hair and not a worry in the world. And sometimes, to borrow from Axl Rose, it's the cold November rain.

Life is an undulating journey of ups and downs. But whatever life throws at you, whatever your rock bottom looks like, this book will help you navigate it. Help you build resilience. Help you cope with the not-so-good times. And, importantly, help you appreciate the good times.

WHAT ROCK BOTTOM LOOKED LIKE FOR NICHOLAS

Dover, England, 2009. A single guy living in a crappy, depressing flat. A lot of broken dreams.

Before this point, I (Nicholas) had been building a successful career in property. I'd worked hard to build a portfolio of rental properties and developments that were bringing in a very nice level of income each month. I wasn't wildly rich, but I'd achieved a moderate level of success and had big plans for the future. I was well on my way. Or so I thought.

Then the financial crisis happened. The resulting credit crunch meant property sales fell off a cliff and funding dried up. I had to liquidate most of the assets I'd worked so hard to gain, leaving me with three small rental properties. After covering the mortgage on those properties, there was just enough income left over each month to keep my head above water. I was broke, but not bankrupt. Depressed, but not destitute. Some people had it much worse than me. But it was a big step back.

Which is how I found myself renting a crappy flat in Dover (it was very cheap). And driving a knackered old Peugeot 106 that I'd bought for £100. As a car lover, that stung almost as much as losing my properties. (I'm joking. Mostly.)

Going backwards like that just as my career was supposed to be taking off ... well, it felt almost like a kind of grief. I was grieving the material comforts and financial security that I'd lost. But more than that, I was grieving the future I *should* have had.

So I dreamed up a better future. And I went on a journey of self-improvement, gathering the mindset tools I'd need to help me climb out from rock bottom, and build a better life for myself. Not just get back to where I was, but build something new.

That was the gift rock bottom gave me. I might not be where I am today - multi-millionaire property expert, educator, and TV presenter - if I hadn't experienced that low. And of course, life has thrown other challenges and lows my way over the years. That's life for you. But I've always been able to fall back on the lessons I learned from my own rock bottom.

MARTIN'S ROCK BOTTOM WAS ALSO AN OPPORTUNITY IN DISGUISE

This book started at a time when I (Martin) was at my very own rock bottom.

The life that I had taken for granted for so long had come crashing down around me. It was sudden, it was abrupt, it was unexpected and, if I'm honest, it was devastating. I know what it's like to experience despair, anger, fear, and sadness. I understand the range of emotions that a person goes through at rock bottom. Most of all I understand how difficult it is to see rock bottom as an opportunity, especially when you're in that dark place, because that is exactly where I was.

I also know that, so often, opportunity will appear exactly when you need it most. For me it was by way of my co-author Nicholas. We had often spoken of writing something together, but the stars had yet to align. Yet as we spoke, we realised that both of us, in our own way, was experiencing our own version of rock bottom. More importantly, we realised that, almost subconsciously, we were both using similar tools for support and to work our way through. It was from this place that *The Rock Bottom Paradox* was born.

You could say this book was written for a very selfish reason. I'd love to say that I started writing this book with you the reader in mind. That I started with some grand intention to better the world, to help others, to share some profound knowledge, to change lives, to teach and to guide. The truth is I can't.

Because this book was a form of catharsis, a way of picking myself up from my own rock bottom. It was my personal blueprint for turning adversity into opportunity. Why am I telling you this? Because I want you to know that the blueprint in this book has been tested, and that it works. I want you to know that someone else does understand what you're going through, has been through it, and has come out the other side. Most of all I want to let you know that it's all okay, how you're feeling is normal, and that no matter how difficult it all feels now, it will get better.

A NOTE ABOUT THE AUTHOR VOICE IN THIS BOOK

Since this book is part of the Extraordinary Millionaire series, the 'I' voice that you hear in the rest of this book is the Extraordinary Millionaire. The Extraordinary Millionaire is both of us, Nicholas and Martin. Sometimes he's more Nicholas, and sometimes he's more Martin, but this book was born from both of our experiences. Both of us are enormously passionate about helping others and passing on the mindset tools that have helped us navigate adversity. Both of us are living proof that the techniques in this book really do work.

Both of us have been Extraordinary Millionaires, achieving great successes in life. And as you already know, both of us have been at rock bottom. To put it another way, we've both been the person on top, giving out life advice from a position of privilege, and we've both been the person at the bottom, on the receiving end of much-needed advice and support.

Safe to say, we've both been Bill at some point in our lives, which is how we're able to tell his story.

WHO'S BILL?

This book takes a storytelling approach. And every good story needs a hero.

Bill is the hero of our story. He may be a fictional hero, but he's very much rooted in our real-life experiences.

Bill's story is one you may be familiar with yourself - a middle-aged person whose life appears to be perfectly on track, then it comes crashing down overnight. Bill finds himself lost, directionless, and completely at sea. He has to learn how to be himself again. How to identify what he really wants from life. We'll follow Bill on this journey - from rock bottom, to preparing for the climb up, to being on the climb itself, and the lessons he learns for the rest of his life.

In each chapter, we'll check in with Bill at a different stage of his journey, and then we'll pull out the practical lessons that you can apply, based on Bill's experience.

WHAT IS AN EXTRAORDINARY MILLIONAIRE?

We won't dwell too much on the topic of the Extraordinary Millionaire because this book isn't about growing your wealth. It's about healing and building resilience and overcoming life's challenges. But since this book forms part of the Extraordinary Millionaire series, we want to briefly explain what we mean by 'Extraordinary Millionaire'.

The Extraordinary Millionaire is both a mental attitude and a methodology. A way of raising yourself up as you raise up those around you. A means of setting exciting goals that drive you forward, but also being thankful and present *right now*. It's a pathway to prosperity. Not the *only* pathway to prosperity. But we believe it's the best one.

For more on the Extraordinary Millionaire series, see 'What to read next' at the end of the book.

THINK OF THIS BOOK AS A BLUEPRINT

Because this book follows the whole story, from Bill hitting rock bottom to coping with adversity and then creating a better life, it's a bit like a roadmap. But we've always referred to this book as a 'blueprint'. A blueprint for navigating adversity and reimagining your life.

It's designed to be a quick read - hence the storytelling approach - but also something that you can refer to time and time again. Because the climb from rock bottom isn't a straight-up affair. There will be times when you go sideways or you feel like you're on a downward slope. That's okay. It's life. With this book, you know you can always fall back on your rock bottom blueprint - your plan for getting out from rock bottom and working towards the life you desire.

One thing we'll talk about in this book is that successful people aren't afraid of rock bottom. They don't fear failure. Why? Partly it's because they know that failing is part of learning. But it's also because they know they have the tools they need to get out, to rebuild something even better. Knowing that you have this blueprint may give you more confidence for the future - because when things don't go to plan (as inevitably some things won't), you know you have the necessary tools right here in these pages.

Bottom line, our hope is you'll reread this book whenever you're going through a tough time. Read it over and over again. Highlight passages. Scribble in it. This is YOUR blueprint.

Now, let's meet our hero Bill, just as he hits his version of rock bottom...

Part I: The Bottom

FINDING ACCEPTANCE AND STRENGTH WHERE YOU LEAST EXPECT IT

'No one ever told me that grief felt so like fear.'

–C S LEWIS

Chapter 1

FACING YOUR LOSS (WHATEVER IT MAY BE)

My friend Bill had it all. Until the day he didn't.

It had started as a perfectly normal day. Getting his daughter, Callie, up and ready for school. Checking emails. Eating breakfast as the sun streamed through the kitchen windows. Thinking about the day and week ahead.

That's the thing about rock bottom. Sometimes you see it coming. You *feel* yourself gradually slipping down towards it. And sometimes it comes out of the blue. The ground drops away and you thud down into the basement of your life.

For Bill, it was one of those ground-falling-away moments. His wife of 15 years announced that she wanted a divorce. Then she walked out the door, leaving Bill thinking, Wait, what the hell just happened?

He didn't see it coming, and he was totally unprepared. But there he was, at rock bottom, desperately trying to figure out what he was supposed to do now.

Bill and I had been friends for several years by this point. We had met at a business networking group years ago and had even invested in one or two properties together. Although Bill had gone a different route to me career-wise, we'd developed a long-lasting friendship. We'd holidayed together. His 12-year-old daughter and my oldest daughter were happy to hang out together. Bill was super-smart, funny, quick to laugh, and incredibly active. The sort of guy who runs ultramarathons for fun. He was loyal, too, a valued friend. If I ever needed anything - anything at all - Bill would be top of my list of people to call.

Like anyone, Bill had had his fair share of setbacks over the years, including his startup business failing. But he was, in general, used to succeeding in life. After his business failed, he started working for a consultancy firm and quickly climbed the corporate ladder. On paper, his life was what many people aspired to - he had the nice house and cars, a successful career, comfortable finances, long marriage, happy child. He had it all. And then one day he didn't.

THERE ARE MANY TYPES OF GRIEF

When I saw him a few days after the bombshell, I was surprised at how hard he was being on himself.

'It's all the crying,' Bill shook his head. 'I mean, I can hold it together when Callie is around, obviously. But the second I'm on my own, it's like the floodgates open and I can't stop. I didn't know it was possible for someone to cry so much and not die of dehydration.' He managed a laugh.

'It's okay,' I reassured him. 'It's a normal part of grief.'

Bill almost grimaced at the word 'grief'. 'I don't know,' he said. 'It's not like anyone died. This is awful, sure, but I can't compare it to actual grief. There are people out there going through much worse.'

'Grief is what you feel after a loss,' I said. 'And that's exactly what you're going through. You've lost something huge. So don't be hard on yourself for grieving that loss. It's a natural ... no, it's a *necessary* process.'

Bill was not alone in shying away from the word 'grief'. In my experience, most people only associate grieving with the death of a person or a cherished pet. But grief is simply about loss. And that loss could be anything - a relationship, a job, a home, a long-held dream, robust health, or anything you hold dear. Something is over, something is lost, something has changed. It hurts. Grief is an important part of the healing process.

I relayed this to Bill and he thought for a moment.

'Well, that does explain all the denial,' he said. 'That's one of the stages of grief, right? Denial? I keep telling myself this isn't really happening. That she doesn't mean it, and she'll be home soon, and we'll go back to normal. I *know* this is happening, of course, I'm not delusional. But it's like I can't accept it. My brain wants to fight this version of reality. Because, if I accept it, then what? This is my life now?'

From what I'd heard from my wife, who had been in contact with Bill's wife, there was no chance of reconciliation.

'Yes,' I said. 'This is your life now. But you won't always feel this way. Look, I've not been through what you're going through, but I've hit my own rock bottom. I've been down in that hole. I survived. I climbed back up. And so will you.'

Bill nodded firmly, as though he was reassuring himself as much as me, 'I know. I know.'

'Have you considered talking to a therapist or grief counsellor?' I asked.

'I don't know what good that would do,' Bill sighed. 'It's not going to make her come back.'

'No,' I agreed. 'But like I said, grieving is part of healing. Maybe if you spoke to someone who specialises in this sort of thing, they could give you some pointers on how to navigate it?'

'I'll think about it,' he promised.

As he showed me to the front door, Bill asked, 'Am I ever going to feel okay again?'

'Yes,' I said without a moment's hesitation. 'I'm going to tell you what I wished someone had said to me when I was at my lowest. "It's going to be okay. You are *allowed* to feel this way. It's normal. And you're not alone."'

ACCEPTANCE IS A VITAL STEP ON THE ROAD TO RECOVERY

A couple of weeks later I met Bill for a walk. Fresh from his first session with a grief counsellor, he looked physically lighter. Tired, but lighter.

'So how was it?' I asked.

'Messy,' he laughed. 'If I thought the floodgates had opened before, they *really* opened in that room.'

'Oh yeah?'

He explained, 'For the first time ever, I allowed myself to talk about the losses I'd experienced, from my parents' divorce and how that made me feel about my own separation, to the death of my father. Things I'd never really spoken about. Things I'd never allowed myself to speak about before. I didn't realise quite how much I'd been bottling up.'

'And what did the counsellor say?'

'For the most part, she just sat there and listened while I poured it all out. But she said that it was normal and that it was good to let it out. We talked about the stages of grief – did you know there are seven of them? There used to be five, but now there's seven. And they can happen in any order, even at the same time.'

I nodded. I knew from experience that it was perfectly possible to be in denial about something happening and at the same time angry about the thing I was in denial about! Bill had it right: grief is messy.

He continued, 'She said something that really stuck with me. She said that grief wasn't about saying goodbye or *getting over* my marriage ending; it's about accepting that something that was – my marriage – no longer is. Simple as that. I need to accept that loss before I can move forward onto the next phase of my life.'

'Accepting the fact that the past is the past?'

'Exactly,' he agreed. 'And that this, the present, is my new normal. Once I accept that, I can lay the foundation for tomorrow and the day after that and the day after that. Grief is like laying the groundwork for the future, essentially.'

'Sound advice,' I said. 'She didn't happen to fill you in on the secret to acceptance, did she?'

He smiled. 'Not exactly.'

'Ah.'

'Turns out acceptance comes at the end of the grieving process. There's no shortcut to it, and you can't fake it. You have to do the work, feel the feelings, and move through the stages.' He shrugged, 'Which is what I'm doing, so that's good.'

'But you feel better having spoken to her?' I asked. 'And you'll go back?'

'Oh definitely,' he said. 'Just the sense of relief from letting go of all the things I was unconsciously holding onto... it was intensely powerful. I know there's a long road ahead, but I feel ... hopeful isn't the right word. More confident, maybe. There's comfort in trusting the process, you know?'

'Absolutely, I do.'

EVERYONE'S ROCK BOTTOM IS DIFFERENT

My rock bottom wasn't one of those ground-dropping-away moments, like it was for Bill. And my loss wasn't the loss of a marriage. It was the loss of a dream. I was young, in my early twenties, and hungry for success. I'd long dreamed of being a successful entrepreneur and living an abundant, happy life. But the reality was I was living in a crappy flat in Dover, broke, absolutely miserable and with no easy way out. This wasn't how it was supposed to be. My mental health was through the floor. It was the lowest I'd ever felt.

Rock bottom sort of crept up on me. There was no dramatic soap-opera moment. No lightning-bolt moment of realisation that this - *this* - was my low point and that the only way from here was up. (Don't you hate it when people offer that platitude?) No, my rock bottom was a period of time, a phase of my life. I didn't think of it as grieving, but I look back and can see I went through some of the stages, like denial ('I'm not that broke. Everything is fine') and anger ('Why is this happening to me?'). I certainly went through depression and felt lonely.

The turning point came when I accepted that the life I'd dreamt of hadn't come to pass, as yet. But that I was in control of my future. No one else was going to drag me from my rock bottom. It was up to me and me alone. Like Bill, I took comfort in the process and knew that if I worked on myself - set myself goals, worked on my mental health, worked on my personal education, worked on income strategies, and so on - I would climb up and achieve the life I dreamed of. And I did.

That's not to say there haven't been other lows. I've had businesses fail, lost relationships, and lost a beloved parent. The journey up from rock bottom isn't like scaling a mountain - it's more like scaling a range of mountains. There will be times when you're climbing, times when you're plateauing and times when you have to go down before you can go back up. You might arrive at what you think is a summit, only to find there's a gnarlier ascent ahead that you didn't even know was there!

I don't say that to put you off. The climb is absolutely worth it. (I mean, who wants to hang out at rock bottom forever? It's damp down there and there's that weird basement smell.) I just wanted to emphasise that it might not be all up-up-up.

Bill's journey would be different to mine, of course. We'll follow his journey throughout this book. But for now, let's explore your own healing process.

FACING YOUR LOSS

Grief is universal. And yet it's so uniquely personal.

It's also not a linear process. Bill's counsellor told him that acceptance is the final stage of grief. But I'd argue there's an earlier form of acceptance – accepting the very fact that what you're going through *is* loss. Bill didn't immediately recognise that what he was experiencing was loss. Do you? It may not be loss in the sense of a death. It may simply be the end of something in your life.

We don't talk very openly about loss in our society. When people ask how we're doing, we say, 'Fine thanks, you?' even if we're not fine. I believe we should change this. I'm a naturally upbeat person who likes to focus on the sunny side of life, but I still believe we should be able to say, 'Actually, I'm struggling a bit today. Tomorrow is another day, but today I'm not doing so good.'

And when someone we know is having a tough time, how quick we are to say things like, 'Everything will be alright' and 'chin up.' Most of the time we're uncomfortable with our own sadness, let alone other people's. So we rush to gloss over it, offering up the things that people always say. We almost stigmatise loss and see it as something to 'get over' as quickly as possible.

Perhaps what we should be saying is, 'Everything will be alright, *once you've healed.*'

Acceptance. Healing requires acceptance and facing up to your situation *as it is now*. Only then can you begin the journey from rock bottom – whatever rock bottom looks like to you – towards the life you desire.

Bill started his journey that day in the park, after his first counselling session. When he gave himself permission to mourn the future that he'd lost. That was Bill's first step towards a new future. Not the future he originally had in mind, but a future worth striving for nonetheless. His feelings of loss were vital preparation for that journey. They would, unexpectedly, give him strength.

But as I said, this not a linear process or a linear journey. There are several stages to the grieving process - or as I'd like to call it from here on in, *the healing process* - and they may not occur in a neat order.

TRUST THE PROCESS

Healing isn't about forgetting, glossing over how you feel or 'getting over' something. As Bill's counsellor said, it's about coming to terms with your situation and accepting that what has happened has happened.

Psychiatrist Elisabeth Kübler-Ross set out the five stages of grief in her 1969 book *On Death and Dying* (although, as we know, these stages may be applied to any type of loss). Since then, two more stages have been added to try and better reflect the complexities of loss.

But before we get into the seven stages, it's important to note that the healing process will be entirely personal and unique to each person reading this book. Kübler-Ross's original model attracted some criticism from people who assumed the stages were an exact roadmap of what everyone should go through, and in a set order. But that's not the case. Yes, there will be commonality between experiences, but your feelings are yours. In your version of rock bottom, you may not experience all of these stages. You may not experience them in the order set out below. You may experience multiple stages at once. You may experience a particular stage more than once. Some stages may pass very quickly while others seem to linger much longer. It's all normal. All of it.

There's no right or wrong way to do this, basically. The only way you can really go wrong is to ignore your feelings or situation. As Bill put it, you have to trust the process and feel the feelings if you're to arrive at a place of acceptance.

You might be wondering, then, if the stages are so unpredictable or may not even happen to you, why you need to know about them. Well, I believe that by knowing about them, you stand a better chance of recognising them, if and when they arise. Bill later told me that he experienced some of the stages more than once, but because he and his therapist had talked about the grief stages, he was much better prepared when he found himself repeating a phase.

Most importantly, you can take some comfort in the fact that what you're feeling is perfectly normal. As I said to Bill that day, you're not alone.

RECOGNISING THE SEVEN STAGES

So let's explore these seven stages of grief – or, as I prefer, healing:

1. Shock and denial

For many, this is an especially intense phase. As well as feelings of shock and denial, you may also experience physical symptoms such as nausea or lack of appetite. You may even feel waves of panic creep up on you as you try to process the situation you find yourself in.

Bill spent the early days of his separation reassuring himself that it was nothing more than 'a blip'. That there was no way his wife would break up their family. At the root of his utter disbelief, he just didn't want to accept that his marriage was over. On top of this he would experience very real physical symptoms, especially right at the beginning, like shaking hands, a dry mouth and an inability to sleep. And then as the physical symptoms faded, he would often find himself staring into space, feeling nothing. It was almost like he was watching it all happen to someone else. 'Numbness' is a common word used to describe this stage.

2. Pain and guilt

And then, as the shock and denial fades, the emotional (maybe even physical) pain of loss makes its presence known. With that, comes guilt. You may find yourself wondering whether you could or should have done something different (even if your rational brain knows otherwise).

For Bill, this was the worst phase to go through as he beat himself up with 'what ifs'. What if he had tried more, given more, paid more attention... He blamed himself. The turning point came when he began to distinguish between blame and responsibility. He wasn't to blame. It was no one's fault. It was just over. But he could take responsibility for his thoughts and actions, now and moving forward. It may help to understand that you, too, are responsible for how you respond to your thoughts and feelings. And, crucially, that you are *not* responsible for the actions of others.

3. Anger and bargaining

It's entirely normal to feel angry when you find yourself at rock bottom. Angry, frustrated, and ready to snap at a second's notice. This anger may be directed at yourself, at someone who has 'wronged' you, at the world, or even at some higher power. And, let's be honest, it will also be directed at entirely innocent people who cross your path or say the wrong thing.

Oh boy, was Bill angry. Angry with his wife and himself. Angry with other people for being happy. (How dare they!) Even angry with the sun for rising in the morning after another long night with no sleep.

This stage may or may not be accompanied by bargaining. You may think things like, 'If only I could have a second chance/another day with that person/another opportunity to prove myself, it would all be okay.' The unlikely combination of bargaining and explosive anger can make this stage feel like you're on an emotional rollercoaster.

4. Depression, loneliness, and reflection

This is generally when reality begins to set in, as you reflect upon what has happened and how your life may change. It really starts to sink in. And as such, you may feel sad, depressed, lonely or hopeless. It's normal to want to withdraw into yourself and deal with these feelings alone - and to some extent it's good to have time to yourself to process things. But it's also important to lean upon your support network and allow people to help you.

Bill certainly felt that urge to withdraw from the world. He didn't want to talk to people or do anything. He would spend his evenings replaying scenarios in his head and, consequently, this was when Bill was most likely to re-enter earlier stages, like denial.

On a practical note, Bill found that forcing himself to go on short walks on his lunchbreak was surprisingly impactful. It gave him space to think more clearly and process his feelings. And no matter how down he felt at the start of the walk, just being outside in nature was helpful, and he would always return from his walk feeling a little better.

5. The upward turn

Gradually, all the feelings associated with the earlier stages will become less intense. They may or may not go away entirely, but they will feel less dominant. This is the start of the upward turn.

Bill knew he was entering the upward turn when his thoughts started to shift away from what he could not change, towards the things he could change. When he thought of the future, he no longer thought about the future he'd lost, but that his future could be anything he wanted it to be. One day, he woke up and decided - a literal, conscious decision - that his future was in his hands. It was up to him to build the life he wanted.

6. Reconstruction

At this point, you may begin to feel more control over your life and circumstances again. Thoughts of the future may no longer seem daunting - there may even be a flicker of excitement.

Bill occasionally experienced some of the earlier stages at this point, and you might too. But most importantly, he felt back in the driving seat of his own life. He no longer felt that things were happening *to him*.

7. Acceptance and hope

This final stage doesn't mean that you're 'over it' or are content to be at rock bottom. But by this point you are able to acknowledge what has happened without emotionally falling apart. You feel ready to move forward and face whatever life has in store next.

Finally, Bill came to accept that the life he had planned for his family wasn't going to play out as he expected, but that his future was nonetheless bright. He felt ready to leave rock bottom behind and begin the climb up.

FINDING THE HELP YOU NEED

Bill was lucky to find an awesome counsellor who understood loss and helped him navigate the healing process, with all its twists and turns. Whatever rock bottom looks like to you, there may be value in talking to a professional. It doesn't have to be a grief specialist - you may simply want to talk through feelings of anger, learn some strategies to manage anxiety, or whatever. But if you can seek professional support, do.

Your GP or family doctor may be a good first port of call, although I acknowledge that (certainly in the UK), free mental health services are stretched. You may therefore find yourself on a waiting list. If you're funding your own therapy, online therapy is often more affordable than in-person therapy. Alternatively, you can ask your employer, if you have one, whether they offer therapy via their employee assistance programme.

You could also join a local support group that's relevant to your situation. Or contact the many charities and helplines that exist to listen to people in need, including the Samaritans and the Campaign Against Living Miserably (CALM).

Most importantly, be open with friends and family about how you're feeling. Rock bottom can feel like an isolating place, but almost everyone has experienced their version of rock bottom at one time or another. Lean upon your loved ones as you navigate the journey from rock bottom towards a much better place.

LESSONS FROM ROCK BOTTOM

- Everyone's rock bottom is different. Sometimes you see it coming. And sometimes it comes entirely out of the blue.
- It may seem over-the-top to use the word 'grief' in relation to rock bottom. But grief is simply about loss. And that loss could be anything - a relationship, a job, a home, a long-held dream, robust health, or anything you hold dear. Something is over, something is lost, something has changed.
- Rock bottom hurts, but facing it head-on is an important part of the healing process. You need to feel the feelings, not gloss over them.
- Trust the healing process and its various phases, including anger and denial. At the end comes acceptance - acceptance and acknowledgement that what's done is done. You cannot control what has been, but you can control your future.
- When you're at rock bottom, it's easy to focus on the past. But it's important to accept your present. Because, when you can accept the present, you're ready to move forward and start building the future you desire.

- There's enormous strength in acceptance. This is the start of your journey up from rock bottom.

Many people who find themselves at rock bottom have spent their lives putting others before themselves. Maybe that sounds familiar to you. If so, the next stage of the journey is going to rock your world. Because it's all about accepting who you are and becoming your own priority. Get ready for an injection of self-love and self-belief.

Chapter 2

BECOMING YOUR OWN PRIORITY

You know the saying, 'You have to take care of yourself before you can take care of others'? Well, Bill was learning that lesson the hard way. After years of putting everyone else's needs above his own, he was feeling lost. Directionless.

'I've always measured my happiness by the many roles and responsibilities I'd imposed on myself,' he said. 'Husband, father, breadwinner, boss, son, provider… you know? I never realised just how much I based my own self-worth on meeting other people's needs. I always told myself, if they were happy, then I was happy.'

'And now?' I asked, pouring him a fresh coffee from my flask.

'It's like I've lost a big part of my identity,' he said. 'I don't even know how I feel about myself or what my purpose is anymore. Sounds dramatic, doesn't it?'

'Sounds like you need to learn how to be *you* again. How to take care of your own needs. You know what the safety demo on a flight always says, "You have to fit your own oxygen mask before you can help others."'

'Life advice from EasyJet?' Bill laughed. 'Now I know things are bad.'

We sat looking out over the small fishing lake for a few moments before Bill spoke again.

'I've always thought that sounded pretty selfish, to be honest,' he said. 'The whole putting-your-own-mask-on-first thing.'

I shrugged, 'Sometimes being selfish isn't a bad thing. I'm not talking about being selfish to the extent of having no consideration for others, or hurting other people. In this case, being selfish is simply to recognise that everything starts with you. You can't help someone fit their mask if you're starved of oxygen yourself. You can't help someone be happy if you're not happy yourself. And you can't encourage someone to love you when you don't love yourself.'

SELF-WORTH COMES FROM WITHIN

Bill had been basing his own happiness and self-worth on the happiness of those around him. But there's a fundamental flaw with that approach: you can't *make* someone else be happy. Despite the focus Bill put on his wife's happiness, she just wasn't happy in their marriage.

You cannot control someone else's happiness. You aren't responsible for other people's happiness. The only happiness you can control, and are responsible for, is your own.

That can be a hard lesson to learn after a lifetime of putting others first, as Bill was discovering.

'What does your therapist say about all this?' I asked him.

'She says that if I want the people around me to be happy and satisfied, then I must work to make myself happy and satisfied. She says it's like yawning – it's contagious. Happiness attracts happiness. Love within attracts love without. That sort of thing.'

'Like how it's impossible to keep a straight face around a giggling child, or be sad around a playful puppy?'

'Exactly.'

'So you have to become the puppy?' I laughed.

'Yes,' Bill nodded in fake seriousness. 'My therapist told me to become a puppy. No, she said one of things I could do is focus on responsibility rather than blame.'

'Go on...' I prompted.

'As in, it's easy to fall into the trap of blaming others for how we think and feel. Or blaming ourselves for how *other people* think and feel. Like me blaming myself and saying things like, "it's my fault she wasn't happy." It's a dangerous way to think. It's unhelpful. And it's also not true.'

'Because you can't control how others think and feel.'

'Right,' he said. 'But I can take *responsibility* for my own thoughts, feelings and actions. I can take responsibility for how I react to circumstances. I can take responsibility for the things that I can control - like my future, how I move forward, how I think about myself, how I choose to spend my time, and so on.'

'Which is how we ended up here,' I said, nodding at the fishing lake.

'Exactly. How many times have you invited me fishing and I've turned you down because I felt guilty taking time away from the family on a weekend?'

'About a million,' I said. 'I'm glad you came today.'

'This is exactly what I needed. Some time to myself, without judgement or guilt. And then when I pick Callie up later from her mum's, I'll be in a much better mood.'

WHAT HAPPENS WHEN YOU DON'T PRACTISE SELF-CARE

'I had to do something similar the other week,' I admitted. 'You know I like my meditation, but I've been really slacking off with that lately. What with moving house and the business and the kids' schedules, it's been hard to carve out the time. Sometimes I feel guilty for wanting 15 minutes to myself when everything's so full-on, you know?'

Bill nodded for me to continue.

'So I'd got to the point where I hadn't meditated in, maybe, two months? God, two months. And I was starting to feel frayed around the edges.

Getting a bit irritable, because I hadn't made the time for myself. We were staying in this little holiday chalet. Super-cute, but we were on top of each other. The kids were charging around. It was noisy chaos and I just had to say to my wife, "Do you know what? I have to take 30 minutes out." And I wandered off into the woods, found a quiet bench and just meditated for 15 minutes. It made such a difference. Not just in those moments, but for days afterwards. I was so much calmer and happier having made time for something that's important to me. And I was able to free my wife up to do something nice for herself, while I enjoyed the chaos with the kids. It totally changed how I felt for the rest of the holiday.'

'And if you hadn't done it, you probably would have exploded,' Bill said.

'It wouldn't have been pretty,' I laughed. 'In all seriousness, I'd been neglecting things for a bit too long. I don't want to do that again. I don't want to end up like my mum.'

'How's she doing?' Bill asked.

'Struggling,' I said. 'But it's been that way, in one form or another, for a long time. I love her, but it's obvious she's not happy. She's always put other people first, her whole life. She gave up work to raise me and my brother. She never found a career that she loved. She never took up any real hobbies. It was always about other people. The very opposite of self-care. And now she's at a time of her life when she should be kicking back and enjoying life - you know, nice house, financial freedom, grandchildren, lovely husband in my stepdad - and she can't enjoy it. She's in poor health, suffers with depression, has done on and off for years. She's neglected herself for so long, almost revelled in neglecting herself and putting others first. And in the end, it achieves the opposite of what she wants - our relationship suffers because she's become so negative and tired and worn down.'

'Tragic,' Bill said.

'It is a tragedy,' I agreed. 'It's awful how the kindest, most loving people can end up bitter or frustrated because they never took care of themselves. What's left on the surface doesn't reflect the amazing heart underneath. Well, I don't want that for myself. I'm motivated to do better – not just for myself but also to model a better way for my kids.'

Bill was very quiet and still for a moment. 'I think I was on that path,' he said. 'Like your mum. It's scary to think about.'

'Treat this as a wake-up call,' I warned him. 'Taking care of yourself doesn't make you a bad person. It enables you to be the best version of yourself.'

IT'S NOT JUST ABOUT MENTAL HEALTH

Bill was learning – or, rather, re-learning – how to be comfortable in himself, and how to recognise his own needs. With the help of his therapist, and putting in a lot of effort on his own part, he was working on self-care. But it's fair to say his focus was very much on the mental health and wellness side of things, and as yet didn't extend to his physical health.

A few weeks later, he still wasn't sleeping that well, he'd let his exercise routine slide, and the kitchen bin had become a wasteland of takeaway containers.

'I know, I know,' he said, scraping the remnants of last night's curry into the bin. 'I make an effort to cook for Callie. But when she's at her mum's for the week, my good intentions go out the window. I just can't be bothered for myself.'

'No judgement here,' I said. 'I've been the same. When I've felt depressed, I've eaten junk to make myself feel better. And made excuses not to exercise for weeks or months on end.'

'It doesn't work though, does it?' Bill said. 'I tell myself that ordering another takeaway is "a treat" but I feel rubbish afterwards. And then the next day I give myself permission to not go to the gym because I deserve to take it easy, but then that makes me feel rubbish too.'

'But you're still getting out on your lunchtime walks?' I asked. 'You were doing really well with that.'

Bill grimaced. 'Most days ... well, some days ... alright, more often than not, no, I'm not.' He sighed. 'You know what it's like, I think *I'll just deal with this email, or finish this project,*' then before I know it it's 4pm and time to get Callie from afterschool club.'

At least Bill wasn't a drinker. I'd seen that several times before, when a person hits a low point in life and turns to drink or drugs to mask their discomfort. For Bill - and for myself - crappy food and slacking off exercise was our drug of choice. Others might neglect food entirely and lose weight when they're at a low point. We're all different.

It's easily done. But as Bill said, it's a vicious cycle. Eating. Not eating. Drinking too much. Sitting on the sofa instead of getting some fresh air. We all do these things from time to time. But when it becomes a pattern - when we're overwhelmingly choosing to do the thing that we know isn't in our best interests - it's a problem.

The worst thing is we're so quick to blame ourselves afterwards. Which then only makes us more likely to seek comfort in doing more of the same. Which is exactly what Bill was doing: serving up a big helping of blame and guilt.

'I need to stop being so crap about these things,' he said. 'Get my shit together.'

'What was it you said about blame versus responsibility?' I asked.

'Good point,' he nodded. He put on his best 'grown up' voice and said, 'I cannot change the things that have already happened–'

'–like that takeaway,' I said with a smile. 'What even was that?'

'But I can take responsibility for my future. Starting with tonight's dinner.'

I pulled out my phone, typed a few words, and showed him the screen. 'This might help.'

'One of those meal kit things?' Bill said, suspiciously. 'I *can* cook, you know.'

'You're a great cook, but this'll help with the weeknight routine. Help you take care of you, not just your daughter. It's all about using the various tools at your disposal - mental tools, yes, but also practical tools.'

LEARNING TO LOOK AFTER YOURSELF

As you can probably tell, this part of the journey from rock bottom is all about the self and learning to take care of your own needs.

Many people who find themselves at rock bottom, Bill included, have one of those lightbulb moments, where they realise that they've been neglecting their own needs for a really long time. That could mean physical needs - for example, never taking the time out of a busy day to exercise and make yourself a nourishing meal because you're too busy running around after everyone else. It could mean mental health, like how I begin to feel frayed and uneasy when I neglect my meditation practice. It could even mean neglecting your financial and life goals - say, if you dream of starting your own business, but you end up staying in the rat race to maintain a false sense of 'security'.

It may be years before you notice the consequences of neglecting the self. But I can say from my own family experience that the impact will, inevitably, show itself. If you never take care of the self within, eventually, something has to give. You may end up tired, worn down and depressed, as I'd seen happen to my mother over the decades. You may end up exploding at the people you love. You may even end up physically ill.

I'm not saying that neglecting the self necessarily leads to rock bottom (although it might) - just that there's often a correlation between ignoring your needs (physical, mental, whatever) and finding yourself at a low point in life.

Therefore, an important part of preparing yourself for the journey up from rock bottom is to become your own priority. It's not selfish (or rather, it's a positive form of selfishness). It doesn't make you a bad person to want to take care of your needs. It makes you a good person. By taking care of yourself and doing the things that give you strength and resilience, you're in a much better place to take care of the people you love.

For me, taking care of myself means looking at my needs across various different areas - mental, physical, life and financial goals - and finding strategies to meet those needs.

ACCEPTING YOURSELF AND WHAT YOU NEED

What you need will be different to what I need, so don't take this as a prescriptive roadmap that you must follow. For example, I love meditation for maintaining a calm, positive frame of mind, but it might not be your scene. You might find peace by taking a walk in nature, or sketching, or growing your own vegetables. American yoga guru Adriene Mishler has a catchphrase, 'Find what feels good.' And that's what I invite you to do.

What makes you feel good? What gives you strength? And conversely, what drains your energy and leaves you feeling low? How can you do less of that draining stuff to make space for the more constructive habits? (If that's something you struggle with, welcome to the club. Later in the chapter we'll talk about how to make time for yourself when life is busy.)

I can't stress enough that we're all different. We all have different physical and mental needs. Different life goals and different things that make us happy. Heck, we're built differently on the inside. Some people have low serotonin activity, which impacts their mental health. Some people are born with a sex that doesn't match their gender identity. Some people are left-handed, others right-handed. Some people are raging extroverts while others are introverts. It's just the way we're made.

So while external factors can have a huge impact on how you feel, we must also acknowledge that internal factors will play a role.

My point is it's important to recognise and accept *who you are* as a person. Bill found this to be incredibly difficult. After years of placing his self-worth in the hands of others, he found his self-confidence, self-belief and self-acceptance were almost non-existent. And we're talking about a successful guy with a great career and a happy, healthy child. This outwardly successful person had no sense of who he was anymore. Learning to love and accept himself was one of the hardest parts of his journey.

That's not to say you can't work on certain things that you want to change. I have a naturally busy brain that pings from one thought to another constantly. I know and accept this about myself, but I also work to find moments of mental stillness through meditation and mindfulness. Those practices didn't come naturally to me. I had to learn and work at them.

So by all means identify the areas where you'd like to do better and work to improve yourself. That's what this whole book is about. But also learn to accept and even love the things that you cannot change. Because self-acceptance can be a very powerful tool on the journey from rock bottom - not least because it will help you understand what you need, recognise when you need help, and know when you need to focus on yourself.

LOOKING AFTER YOUR MENTAL HEALTH NEEDS

Throughout this book, we'll explore various techniques and activities that I know improve my mental health. Things like:

- Gratitude and positive affirmations (turn to Chapter 3 for more on this)
- The law of attraction and visualisation (see Chapter 10)
- Helping others along the way (Chapter 12)

Personally, I'm a big fan of meditation and mindfulness. What's the difference, you ask? Well, the two are closely linked. Mindfulness can be a form of meditation, and meditation can be part of living a more mindful life.

In essence, mindfulness is being fully aware of the present. To be mindful is to be aware of your thoughts, feelings and anything else that's going on around you. It's just about checking into the here and now - and as such, you can be mindful at literally any minute of the day. You can drink a glass of water mindfully, just by focusing on the feel of the glass and the taste of the cool water in your mouth.

Meditation, on the other hand, is usually more of a formal practice. Like mindfulness, meditation involves bringing your attention to something - like the body, or the breath, or an object. (For some people, they repeat a specific mantra.)

So, mindfulness is more of a feeling of awareness that you can tap into at any moment. Whereas meditation is a more structured practice that you set aside time for. So if you think sitting and meditating isn't for you, I encourage you to give mindfulness a try instead. It's a very easy way to take a few minutes for yourself.

You can be mindful wherever you are, whatever you're doing and whoever you're with. All you need to do is tune into the present and really focus on how you're feeling in that moment - emotionally and in the body - as well as what's going on around you. It's just about *noticing* more.

So, you can notice the feeling of the water as you stand in the shower in the morning. You can notice the sensation of biting into an apple. You can notice the sound of birds in your garden. Too often we move through life on autopilot - and that can be especially true when we're hyper-focused on other people's needs. Mindfulness will help you turn off that autopilot setting and re-engage with how you feel. Re-engage with your needs.

If you're new to mindfulness, I highly recommend using an app like Headspace, which is designed to guide you towards mindful thinking. Physical practices like yoga or tai chi can also help to promote mindfulness, especially if you're like me and have a very busy mind. The movement gives you just enough to focus on to occupy your brain, yet you're also focusing on the sensations of movement and your breath, which is very mindful.

Or you could try the following super-simple mindfulness meditation, which I use to bring my attention to my breath. I love it because I can do it anywhere at any time. When I felt the world was closing in on that holiday, this was the meditation I turned to.

- Sit comfortably - it could be in a chair, on the floor, on a park bench, wherever - and begin to breathe deeply through your nose. Breathe from the belly, not the chest (meaning, push out your belly as you breathe in and suck in your belly as you breathe out).
- Pay attention to the sensation as the breath moves in and out of your nostrils, and focus on that feeling. Feel the flow of breath in and out. Notice where you feel that breath in your body - in your belly, in your lower back, in your shoulder blades, and so on. Focus on one breath at a time.
- Continue to breathe in and out in this way for five minutes (or longer, if you like).

- If your mind is bombarding you with thoughts, gently redirect your thoughts back to your breath. If you're really struggling, you could count a set number of seconds as you breathe in and out. For example, four seconds in and four seconds out.

DON'T FORGET YOUR PHYSICAL HEALTH

Some people on the journey from rock bottom prioritise their mental health needs but neglect the physical self. That was Bill's experience - he found the need to improve his mental resilience was more urgent. And I can also say from experience that I've often made time for things like meditation and gratitude, but gone months without exercising. We're all human. But you can't improve one aspect without the other. Feeling strong mentally supports the physical body, and vice versa - when you're taking care of your body, your mind is more likely to be in better shape.

Be honest, do you make enough time for physical movement? If not, the easiest way to move more is to just make it part of your everyday activities. Could you, for example, cycle to an appointment instead of driving there, or park a little further from the office so you can get more steps in? I've found that small, common-sense habits like these can really build up over time and contribute to a more active lifestyle.

In terms of how much exercise you should aim for, UK government recommendations say at least 150 minutes a week, which is roughly 20 minutes a day. That's easy enough to achieve just by walking a little further to get your lunchtime sandwich.

But more important than quantity, in my opinion, is to find the physical activities that you actually enjoy. If you hate the gym, don't bother taking out gym membership - it's a waste of money! Take up jogging instead. Or wild swimming. Or tennis lessons. Or get a dog...

It's also fun to think back to the kinds of sports you enjoyed when you were a child. I know someone who rediscovered a love of roller-skating in her forties, and now straps on her skates a few nights a week. Another joined adult ballet classes. What's your equivalent? Skipping, maybe, cycling, hula-hooping, trampolining? If you can find some sort of activity that you love, you'll be much more motivated to do it.

Of course, what we put into our body also matters a great deal. I'm not here to tell you what you should and shouldn't eat and drink. To eat well is to eat without restriction or guilt - it's to eat a little of whatever you fancy. As Michael Pollan, author of *In Defense of Food* so neatly put it, 'Eat food. Not too much. Mostly Plants.' And if that includes opening a bottle of wine on a Friday night, that's fine too. (It's made from grapes, after all!)

The key, I think, is to eat a *variety* of foods, stick to whole foods wherever possible, and avoid ultra-processed foods - at least for 90% of the time. (A good rule of thumb is, if the list of ingredients on a packet includes stuff your grandmother wouldn't recognise as real food - preservatives, emulsifiers, and so on - it's a good sign that the product is ultra-processed.)

My friend Bill loved to cook from scratch, but simply wasn't motivated to cook when he was at a low ebb. If that sounds familiar, keep it simple. Cook a big batch of something on Sunday evening that will get you through the first few days of the week. Prep or buy helpful things that you can pull out of the fridge and assemble - like pre-cooked grains and proteins, and chopped veggies. A meal kit service, where they send you the recipe and pre-portioned ingredients, is another great option - and is often pretty affordable compared to the cost of groceries and takeaways these days.

HOW'S YOUR SLEEP?

Not great, I bet. Sleep is often one of the first things to suffer when you're stressed or at a low point in life. That was certainly the case for Bill, who would lay awake at night thinking about 'what ifs' or worrying about the future.

But it's a vicious cycle because poor sleep contributes to poor physical and mental health, which then reinforces the poor sleep. Not getting enough sleep is linked to all sorts of issues, including high blood pressure, weaker immune system, and depression. Medical studies have even shown that lack of sleep can increase the risk of an early death. Therefore, part of prioritising yourself is *prioritising your sleep*.

The question is, how much sleep is enough? Everyone's ideal amount of sleep is different. The National Sleep Foundation recommends adults get seven to nine hours of sleep a night, and I find that eight hours is ideal for me, but you might be different. It doesn't matter so much what your magic number is, what matters more is that you stick to that number and make it a part of your routine.

That means I aim for my eight hours every night - regardless of what's going on and how busy I am. And because routine is so important, I stick to the same amount of sleep on weekends too, rather than sleeping in late. For the most part, then, I go to bed and get up at roughly the same time, even on weekends.

'That must be nice,' I hear you say. 'But I've got young kids who keep me up at night.' Well, I've been there too. My wife and I have three children and we had our fair share of sleepless nights (make that years). But if I'm honest, we also did a lot of the things that everyone knows are terrible for sleep. The things you're not supposed to do. I'd be scrolling on my phone or answering emails late at night. We didn't have proper blackout curtains in our rooms, so we'd all get woken up super-early in summer. We went to bed and got up at different times across the week. We'd eat and drink the wrong things late at night. And then the kids would wake us up and compound what was already going to be a crappy night's sleep.

Bottom line, even when you have kids - or other external factors that interfere with your perfect eight hours of sleep - you can still work to build better sleep habits. For me and my family, that includes:

- I have what I call a 'wind-down routine' that starts one hour before I go to bed. Designed to calm my brain so I can drop off more easily, this hour is a strict 'no screen' time, meaning no phones or tablets. Our kids also have their own wind-down, no-screen rule one hour before their bedtime.
- I start that wind-down hour at pretty much the same time every evening.
- At the start of my wind-down hour, I have a calming herbal tea. (Others swear by hot milk.) I also try to avoid alcohol or rich food in the run-up to that hour.
- On those evenings when I'm feeling particularly stressed, or I'm feeling really alert and not the slightest bit sleepy, I turn to meditation or mindfulness. Just five minutes of calm before bed can help me wind down.
- And when I'm in bed, I spend two or three minutes reviewing my day, thinking about what went well and what I'm grateful for from the day. (We'll talk more about gratitude in the next chapter.) I find that this helps to mentally 'wipe the slate clean'.
- Then, I'll pick up whatever book I'm into and read for a little while. Most nights, thanks to my wind-down routine, it's not long before my eyelids start to feel heavy.
- If I do happen to wake up in the night, I get up and go downstairs, make myself a drink and maybe eat a banana. (Bananas contain magnesium, which relaxes the muscles.) I might also do a brief meditation before going back to bed. Whatever you do, don't reach for your phone.
- I try to avoid snoozing the alarm in the morning, because it only leads to rushing around later. It's really important to give yourself plenty of time in the morning to do all the things you need to, including having a decent breakfast, and, ideally, having a little time to yourself (for meditation, exercise, or whatever you like).
- I've also made physical changes to the whole family's bedrooms to promote good sleep – specifically, fitting blackout blinds or curtains, buying alarm clocks (instead of us all using our phones as alarms), and investing in quality mattresses and pillows.

If you want to really delve into the importance of sleep, I highly recommend reading *The Sleep Revolution* by Arianna Huffington.

UNDERSTANDING YOUR LIFE AND FINANCIAL GOALS

When I found myself at rock bottom, broke and living in that flat in Dover, the root of my problem was that my life and financial situation was so far removed from my goals (life goals and financial goals). Obviously, that disconnect had a noticeable impact on my mental and physical health, but the underlying cause was neither physical nor mental - it was simply that I wasn't living the life I wanted.

In other words, while it's vitally important to honour your mental and physical needs, you must also honour your life and financial goals. If you're working 60 hours a week to service a big mortgage when, actually, having the big status house isn't that important to you, then you're not honouring your values. You're not honouring the things that are most important to you. Alternatively, if you find yourself struggling financially, longing for a far more prosperous life - as I was in my twenties - you are equally not honouring the things that matter to you. You're not prioritising yourself and your needs.

We've talked a lot about taking care of yourself in this chapter. But for me, one of the best ways to take care of yourself (physically, mentally, financially) is to escape the rat race. To stop working to make *other people rich* and build a more prosperous, abundant life for yourself and your loved ones. Therefore, an important part of your journey from rock bottom may involve improving your finances, building wealth, and creating a successful business of your own.

That's the subject of my book *The Extraordinary Millionaire: Harness the REAL tools for success, grow your wealth and build an extraordinary life*. If you haven't read that book, don't worry (although I obviously urge you to read it). We'll touch on some of the major success-building techniques in this book, including:

- Finding your why and setting goals (see Chapters 5 and 6)
- Becoming a lifelong learner (Chapter 7)
- Building a strong network around you (Chapter 11)

HOW DOES ANYONE FIND TIME FOR ALL THIS?

Here's the kicker: even when we know we need to prioritise our own needs, it can be really bloody difficult to find the time. Or the motivation. Because, sometimes time itself isn't the issue - if we're honest, most of us can find 20 minutes out of even the busiest day to do something for ourself - it's a lack of motivation that prevents us doing the things that we know serve us.

Chapter 11 is all about how to stay motivated on this journey towards a better life. But one of the best things you can do is create a routine for the things that matter. Like taking a walk every Monday to Friday in your lunchbreak. Or doing 10 minutes of gentle yoga first thing in the morning. Or going to the same watercolour painting class on Tuesday evenings. Or getting in a habit of batch-cooking some nutritious meals on Sundays.

And listen, I'm just as human as you are. I don't always find time to meditate even though I know it's important to me. I also love writing books and helping people on their own journey - yet, finding the time to write when work is manic can be a real challenge. I'll often catch myself prioritising other tasks, and I have to remind myself that an hour of writing is a much better investment in myself and my future.

Again, routine is key. Try to carve out time for the things that matter to you, even if that means you have to block out the time in your calendar and set yourself reminders. One person I know even sets herself regular reminders on her phone that just say 'Breathe'. It sounds silly but it's a useful reminder to take a few deep breaths and tune into the present moment. Read more about routine in Chapter 7.

And if you have the spare cash, use it to support the things that matter to you. Hire a personal trainer to help you stay committed. Pay for classes that inspire you. I found that working with a life coach made a dramatic difference to my life, but I'll talk more about that in the next chapter. These days, you can even hire an accountability coach (yes, it's a real job title). This is someone who'll help you identify your goals and hold you accountable - basically, they make sure you do the things you say you want to do.

ONE SIMPLE STEP – TRY KEEPING A THOUGHT JOURNAL

Something that really helped Bill was keeping a thought journal. Every time he read or heard something relevant - something that would inspire him towards self-acceptance and self-care - he would jot it down in his journal. Gradually, Bill began to add his own thoughts.

The simple process of writing these things down, and, crucially, re-reading those words on a regular basis, began to rewire his brain towards self-acceptance and love.

He showed me the journal one day and I was deeply touched by what I saw. There were passages like:

- 'No one else is responsible for my happiness.'
- 'I am successful for me and nobody else. I can always share my success with others, but the purpose is for me.'
- 'I will make a better life.'
- 'Whatever happens I will discover a new and wonderful part of myself.'
- And even scrawled on one page were the words, 'Don't worry, be happy.'

Why not try creating your own thought journal? It could be a physical journal or using a notes app in your phone. (If you go for a physical notebook, buy yourself a beautiful notebook. Something you genuinely want to pick up and write in.) As often as you can, jot down any words that help you on this journey. They could be quotes from famous people you admire. Something you read in a book or heard on TV. Or even your own thoughts about self-acceptance, self-care and how best to honour your needs. You might be surprised at how impactful it is.

LESSONS FROM ROCK BOTTOM

- A vital part of preparing yourself for the journey up from rock bottom is to become your own priority. By taking care of yourself and doing the things that give you strength and resilience, you're better able to take care of the people you love.
- Remember, you can't help someone be happy if you're not happy yourself. And you can't encourage someone to love you when you don't love yourself.
- Accept who you are. Sure, you can work to change the things you want to change, but you must also learn to accept and love yourself as you are right now.
- If you don't practise self-care, you may end up exhausted, burnt out, filled with negativity, or even physically ill.
- Prioritising yourself involves identifying your needs across various different areas - mental, physical, life and financial goals - and finding strategies to meet those needs. This might include practising mindfulness and gratitude, making time to exercise and eat well, building good sleep habits, and building a life that's in line with your goals and values.
- Finding time and motivation for self-care can be a challenge, so it's really important to build these practices into your regular routine. One simple strategy is to keep a thought journal and regularly write down thoughts and phrases that help you stay committed to your journey of self-acceptance and self-love.

I mentioned a couple of times in this chapter that gratitude can be a hugely impactful way of shifting your mind into a more positive gear. And as such, it's a really useful tool to deploy when you find yourself at rock bottom. Because even when life isn't going to plan - scratch that, *especially* when life isn't going to plan - it's important to acknowledge the good things in life. However small they may be. So let's explore the topic of gratitude in more detail...

Chapter 3

FINDING GRATITUDE AND POSITIVITY (EVEN WHEN LIFE KNOCKS YOU BACK)

'Don't worry, be happy,' I said, reading aloud from Bill's thought journal.

'Oh that,' he replied. 'Easily said, isn't it? Not so easily done.'

'I thought writing things down was helping you feel more positive?' I asked.

'It is,' he replied. 'It helps to read these words and phrases back. But sometimes, on the really low days, it feels like the words just bounce off me, without having any effect. Like they're just words and they don't have any real power.'

I frowned at him, concerned.

He closed the journal and placed it back on the kitchen table. 'Like I said, most of the time this stuff really helps me. Just that I sometimes feel like I need ... I don't know, something stronger, more powerful.'

'Have you tried saying the words out loud, like you really believe them?' I asked. 'The old positive affirmations technique?'

Bill shook his head, unsure. 'Positive affirmations?'

WHAT YOU TELL YOURSELF MATTERS

'Yeah,' I opened the journal back up. 'This right here, where you've written, "I will make a better life." That's basically a form of positive affirmation. It's just a short, positive statement that inspires and motivates you. I use these sorts of statements all the time. I even get my kids to use them.'

'Really?'

I pulled out my phone and opened the ThinkUp app, an app that I use to note and record my own positive affirmations.

'Here are some of the ones I use,' I said. 'Things like "Calmness washes over me with every deep breath I take." I use that one when I'm feeling stressed in the moment and need to take a beat. Or there's this one, "I love the life I have whilst I work towards the life of my dreams." I use that as a general way to boost my gratitude and positivity.'

'And with your kids?' Bill asked.

'I encourage them to make up their own simple affirmations like "I am the best version of me" or "I am confident" or "I am loved". Or even specific things to set them up for the day, like "I am prepared for today's test". It's just a way of tuning your brain to thoughts that are more positive and constructive, instead of focusing on the things that have gone wrong or could go wrong.'

'And it works for you?' Bill asked.

I nodded. 'The trick is to *believe* the words. Which is why it often helps to say them out loud with conviction. Shout them, even, if you want. And as you say them, you conjure the feelings associated with that statement, as though it's already happened. You can even form a mental picture of it happening.'

'I'm not sure I follow...' Bill said.

'Like, I'm not a particularly confident public speaker,' I said. 'But I often present for YouTube videos and TV, so I need to *feel* like a confident public speaker. Otherwise, I'll just be a bag of nerves. So I'll say to myself something like, "I am a confident presenter" while feeling as if I've already done an amazing job presenting something to camera. I summon up the feeling as though it's already happened.'

Bill nodded. 'So instead of just reading "I will make a better life" I should say it out loud, imagine that life, and feel as though I've already achieved it?'

'Exactly,' I said. 'Although I would personally say, "I *am building* a better life." It's just more active and positive. But you can say whatever you like, so long as it's focused on the positive, not the negative.'

'I don't know...' Bill said. 'It's not always easy to conjure up those feelings, as you put it, when you feel like life's kicking you in the guts.'

'I hear you, mate,' I said. 'But if you do this enough, it begins to rewire the brain. It redirects the brain towards more positive thoughts. Think of it this way, if you constantly tell yourself that you're not good enough, how would that make you feel?'

'Like I'm not good enough,' Bill answered, his tone implying a strong 'duh'.

'Right! So why shouldn't the opposite be true? That if you constantly tell yourself that you *are* good enough, you begin to feel like you are. Every single day Michelle Obama asks herself "Am I good enough?" And then she answers herself, "Yes!" She does that because she's figured out an important life lesson: what we tell ourselves matters.'

TAPPING INTO POSITIVITY, EVEN WHEN TIMES ARE TOUGH

Bill had a point, though. Conjuring up positive thoughts and feelings is hard when you're at rock bottom. And yet, rock bottom is when you need positive thoughts and feelings the most.

As Bill would discover, the journey from rock bottom is a hell of a lot easier if you can learn to think like an optimist, even if you're not one.

I'm not talking about sweeping your problems under the carpet, or ignoring the reality of your situation. I'm not talking about denial. I'm talking about learning to focus the mind towards more positive thoughts, instead of focusing on all the things that have brought you to rock bottom, or all the things that could go wrong in future.

With the help of his therapist, Bill was learning to focus his thoughts and energy on the things he could control in life. Want to focus on the things *you* can control? Start with the narrative you tell yourself.

You are in control of the things you say to yourself. And what you say to yourself matters.

Yes, it's hard to tell yourself positive things when life has knocked you back. And yet, even in our darkest moments in life, there are always things to feel positive about. Things to be grateful for.

Even when life is at its darkest, you can find patches of light. They may be big or small, but there are always positive things to focus on. When I was at my own rock bottom, weirdly enough that's when I met my future wife. The love of my life came along when I was at my lowest. The universe sometimes plays funny tricks on us like that. That new relationship gave me something to be grateful for when I needed it most.

So as well as affirmations, gratitude is a powerful way to direct your thoughts in a more positive way.

RECOGNISING WHAT YOU HAVE WHILE YOU WORK TOWARDS THE THINGS YOU WANT

'Since you're already in the habit of writing down your thoughts and affirmations,' I said to Bill, 'why not also write down some things to be grateful for?'

'Funny you should mention that,' Bill said. 'My therapist was suggesting just that. She set me homework of naming a few things every day that I'm grateful for.'

'And?' I prompted.

'Well,' Bill said, 'I'm grateful for stuff that most people are grateful for. I have my daughter. I still have a roof over my head. I have my health. I'm grateful for those things.'

'You sound it,' I laughed.

He laughed too. 'No, I am. Really. It's just that I've tried telling myself that for the past week and, I've got to be honest, it felt good for the first couple of times. But after that, it didn't seem as powerful.'

'You might do better to try and come up with different things each day. Don't get me wrong, the big stuff like health and family is always good, but if you list the same things over and over again it won't have quite the same impact. When I do it, I list all sorts of things. One day I might be grateful that my kids are all happy and doing well. The next, I might be grateful that I bagged an awesome parking space in town.'

Bill snorted with laughter. 'I don't think that's the sort of thing my therapist had in mind.'

'Want to bet?' I said. 'Being grateful for the small things in life can be just as impactful as the big things.'

'So you do this a lot then?' Bill asked. 'I didn't know that.'

'I try to start and end each day by naming three things I'm grateful for. I keep a notebook next to my bed to write them down. It's amazing the difference it makes. And the brilliant thing is, the more grateful you are, the more you find to be grateful about. It's like a snowball effect.'

'With respect, though' Bill said. 'You have an awful lot to be grateful for in life. Everything's coming up roses for you.'

'You never know what's going on under the surface,' I said. 'A few years after I got married, we were living in Andover by then, we were in a nice enough house and my property career was doing okay, but I still hadn't found that breakthrough success I'd been craving for years. I was starting to wonder if I was ever going to build the life I really dreamed of. Mentally, this period of feeling stalled and impatient was as hard, if not harder, than when I'd had almost nothing a few years earlier. And yet, on the surface, it looked as though life was ticking along just fine.'

TREATING GRATITUDE AS A TOOL IN YOUR TOOLBOX

I continued, 'That was when I started working with a life coach, and she's the person who taught me about tools like gratitude and positive affirmations. The law of attraction. Visualisation. All that stuff. I still use these techniques today because they completely changed my mindset and helped me build the life I have now. Techniques like gratitude taught me how to manage my thoughts and feelings, and direct them where I want. Working with a life coach was my version of therapy. It was transformative. And the great thing is, I have these tools in my toolbox to pull out whenever I need them. If I find myself at a low point again, I know gratitude and affirmations will help me maintain a positive mindset. And mindset is most of the battle, you know?'

Bill nodded, 'Tell me about it.'

'I know you're at your rock bottom right now,' I said. 'But trust me when I say this is exactly when you should become more grateful than you've ever been in your life. The more you practise gratitude, the more you'll find to be grateful for. The more you'll be able to focus on hope rather than fear and sadness.'

'Jeez, that sounds good,' said Bill.

I pushed the notebook towards him. 'So be a good boy and do your gratitude homework.'

WHEN GRATITUDE BECOMES SECOND NATURE

When I next saw Bill, it was a couple of weeks later and he was more animated than I'd seen in a while.

'I think I had a breakthrough this week,' he said.

'Oh yeah?'

'I've been writing down my things to be grateful for each morning. Mixing it up with different things each day, big and small, like you suggested. A phone call from a friend. A cuddle with Callie. The weird lack of traffic on the way into the office. That sort of thing.'

'And...?' I prompted.

'And then a few days ago, I wrote down that I was grateful for hitting the bottom. Can you believe that? Grateful for hitting the bottom. Because this is my opportunity to build something new. I feel like I've been stripped back to the core, but maybe that's not the bad thing I've been assuming. What if this is my chance to build a better way forward? Something new and exciting that I never imagined for myself before?'

'I don't doubt it,' I said. 'That's amazing.'

Bill waved me quiet, 'That's not even the real breakthrough. The next day I found myself noticing more things than ever to be grateful for. I found myself saying "thank you" in my head over and over again. I literally woke up and thought "thank you". I thought how thankful I was to be able to walk downstairs on my own two feet and make myself a cup of coffee. It just went on and on like that. Even things that I wouldn't normally look forward to, like meeting with my accountant, I was still able to feel grateful that they gave me their time and expertise.'

I beamed at him in delight. 'You've caught the gratitude bug.'

'It's mad,' Bill continued. 'Here I am, recently separated, my finances are about to be blown apart by the divorce, I lost a parent this last year. And yet I feel genuinely grateful. I feel like I've unlocked some secret, incredible tool.'

'That's because you have.'

Now let's explore how you can use gratitude and positive affirmations to tune your own thoughts to a more positive frequency. Because when you're able to focus the mind on positive thoughts - even when life isn't going how you want - you're likely to notice more things to feel good about.

HOW TO BECOME MORE GRATEFUL

As I told Bill, I learned about gratitude as a mindset tool from my life coach. And I'm living proof that it works. But you don't have to work with a life coach. Gratitude is something you can easily learn and practise yourself. It's something you can tap into at any minute of the day - at *every* minute of the day, even. And best of all, it's free.

To be grateful is simply to notice and appreciate the (little and big) things in life. To feel thankful for what you have and where you are *right now*. Even rock bottom. Rock bottom can be full of opportunity and potential - it is the foundation upon which you build your future. And that, in and of itself, is something to be grateful for.

A simple starting point is to wake up and say "thank you" each morning. Give thanks for the fact that you woke up at all. That you're in a warm and comfortable bed. That the sun is shining. (Or if it's raining, give thanks that you won't have to water your pot plants!)

And throughout the day, whenever something makes you smile or feel good, take a moment to acknowledge it, either to yourself or out loud. If someone did something nice for you, thank them. If something went well, stop and notice it.

Even not-so-positive moments can provide an opportunity to be grateful. When Bill got stuck in traffic taking his daughter to school, for example, he would flip his irritation around and instead feel thankful for the extra few minutes with her. In this way, you can use gratitude as a way to change your point of view. My life coach taught me that instead of thinking 'Why is this happening to me?', I should ask 'Why is this happening *for* me?' In other words, lots of moments - good, bad, big, small - provide an opportunity to practise gratitude. Even when someone pisses me off, I try to remember that this, too, is an opportunity to control how I react. To react from a place of calm not anger. And for that opportunity, I'm grateful. Seriously.

Becoming more grateful is therefore a useful way to train your brain. And you can do this constantly across the day. You can also turn it into a more formal practice - something you do at a certain time of the day, every day - by creating a gratitude journal.

Buy yourself a nice notebook and each evening, write down three things that you're grateful for from the day. These could be anything. Anything at all. You could be grateful that you did a good job on something during the day. Grateful that your partner brought you a cup of tea. Grateful that your toddler learned a new word. To boost your feelings of gratitude even further, try looking back over your gratitude journal regularly.

You can also start each new day by listing three things that you're grateful for. I like to practise gratitude in the morning, to set me up for a positive day, and in the evening as part of my wind-down, pre-bed routine. Sometimes I'll write these things down in my gratitude journal, and sometimes I'll just think them quietly to myself.

Ideally, gratitude should become part of your everyday routine, like remembering to brush your teeth. Try hard to stick to these habits and, over time, it will become easier to find even more things to be grateful for each day. As Oprah Winfrey once said, 'Be grateful for what you have; you'll end up having more.' When you feel grateful for the things you already have in life - no matter how small - you're attracting more good things your way. Whereas, if you only ever focus on the things you *don't* have, you will never be satisfied. (This is known as the 'law of attraction' and we'll talk more about it in Chapter 10.)

Most importantly, remember that gratitude won't make all of your problems go away. It's not a magic pill that will stop anxiety, or depression or uncertainty. But it will help you put everything in perspective and take control of your thoughts. It will help you shine light where there's darkness.

I've personally found that being thankful is also a fantastic way to shut out the noise of everyday life and bring calm in the present. By focusing on the good things in life - as opposed to all the things that have gone wrong or could go wrong - it helps me let go of stresses.

HOW TO USE POSITIVE AFFIRMATIONS

Alongside gratitude, affirmations are one of my favourite ways of training my brain to focus on the positives, rather than the negatives. Even if you're a lifelong pessimist, I promise that affirmations will help you get into a more positive mindset, believe in your ability to build the life of your dreams, and even overcome challenges that may come your way.

As I explained to Bill, an affirmation is just a short, encouraging statement that inspires you, boosts your confidence, and promotes positive feelings. You can make up your own affirmations that are completely unique to you (after all, we all have different motivations and different things that we want to achieve). Or you can borrow and adapt affirmations from people you admire. You can also borrow from the many books, websites and apps that are tailored to affirmations. I personally love the ThinkUp app, because it gives tons of example affirmations, and lets you create your own. You can even record yourself saying your affirmations, so you can play them back in your own voice.

If you're new to affirmations, a good place to start is with simple 'I am' statements that affirm what you want to be or feel. For example:

- I am successful.
- I am happy.
- I am brave.
- I am proud of who I am.
- I am confident.
- I am enough.

You don't have to start your affirmations with 'I am', and you can get really quite specific with what you say. You can create affirmations that tie into specific goals (for example, 'I have the courage to start my own business'), or use general statements that inspire success and make you feel confident (like 'Success flows to me'). The key is to find affirmations that resonate with you, whatever they may be.

Sometimes I'll use affirmations to plan for a successful day, by saying something like 'I am well prepared for this presentation.' Affirmations like this help me to focus on what I want to happen, as opposed to getting bogged down in the things I *don't* want to happen.

And that's one of the keys to making affirmations work - verbalise the things you *want*, not what you *don't* want. Statements like 'I am not a failure' or 'I won't end up lonely' aren't positive; they're extremely negative. Instead, flip those statements around and say something much more assertive and positive, like 'I achieve the things I want' and 'I attract love.'

Write your favourite affirmations down - on post-it notes, in a notebook, or in an affirmation app. Over time, you'll probably amass quite a long list of positive affirmations that you can pick and choose from depending on how you're feeling or what you want to achieve.

Using the ThinkUp app, I've organised my favourite affirmations into categories such as motivation, calm and self-esteem. That way, I can pick from the categories according to how I'm feeling and what I need each day. It's one of the things I love most about affirmations - they're completely flexible, and you can tailor them to suit pretty much any situation.

If possible, try to get into the habit of saying your affirmations at the same time every day, whether that's first thing in the morning, in the shower, or whenever. You can also say them throughout the day whenever you need an injection of positivity. The important thing is to make it part of your daily routine.

It's also important to believe in your affirmations. As I said to Bill, you have to wholeheartedly believe in an affirmation for it to have any real effect. So whatever affirmations you use, try to cultivate those feelings that accompany the words. If you're telling yourself you're successful, conjure up those feelings. If you're telling yourself you are calm, take deep breaths and work on actually *feeling* calm.

Visualisation - basically, forming a mental picture of the thing you desire - can be a really powerful way to conjure up feelings of belief and certainty in your affirmation. We'll talk more about visualisation in Chapter 10.

THE IMPORTANCE OF BEING HUMBLE

Bill once told me that hitting rock bottom is a humbling experience. And I couldn't agree more. Hitting rock bottom is like being stripped back down to basics. But turning that into a positive, rock bottom can change how you see things - it can certainly change what's important in life.

Particularly as you work on gratitude, you might notice that many of the things to be grateful for are the most basic things in life. Relationships. Small kindnesses. Moments that make you smile. They don't require money or status or material goods. Not that it's bad to be grateful for material things – I just mean that finding gratitude in a wider range of things can be incredibly humbling.

I invite you to carry that humility forward on your journey. Because being thankful and being humble go hand in hand. It's really important to stay humble on the way up. To keep hold of your humanity. To remember the basics that you were stripped back to. Because even when you do achieve the life of your dreams, it doesn't make you a better human being than anyone else – just as being at rock bottom doesn't make you a worse human being than anyone else. Staying thankful, staying humble and staying focused on the good things in life are what make you a good person. Not the money or the status or the material things.

There's an old saying that I like to keep in mind: 'Money talks but wealth whispers.' I am wealthy. I'm a multi-millionaire, in fact. But I despise arrogance in rich people. I hate to see successful people flashing their wealth and putting other, less outwardly successful people down. Such people could do with a stint at rock bottom. I know my time at rock bottom made me more grateful and more giving on the way up.

I wanted to stress the importance of humility because some people might mistakenly think that positive affirmations are about inflating your sense of self to the point of arrogance. They're not. They're not designed to make you feel like you're better than everyone else – affirmations are simply designed to tune your brain to more positive thoughts and feelings. The same with gratitude.

Use these tools wisely and I guarantee you'll feel more positive and resilient. And you'll also be in a better place to help others on your way up.

LESSONS FROM ROCK BOTTOM

- The journey from rock bottom will be a lot easier if you can learn to think like an optimist (even if you're not one).
- Positivity isn't about sweeping your problems under the carpet, or ignoring the reality of your situation. Rather, it's about focusing the mind towards more positive thoughts, instead of focusing on all the things that have brought you to rock bottom, or all the things that could go wrong in future. It's about changing your mindset from negative to positive, from dark to light, and from fear to hope.
- There are two really powerful tools that will help you foster a more positive mindset: gratitude and affirmations.
- To be grateful is simply to notice and appreciate the (little and big) things in life. To feel thankful for what you have and where you are *right now* in your life. Even rock bottom.
- To become more grateful, try to notice little things throughout the day to be thankful for. Say thank you in your head or out loud as often as you can. You can also keep a gratitude journal and list things each day that you're grateful for. It's especially powerful if you can find different things each day.
- Positive affirmations are short, inspiring statements that help you feel more positive and confident. You can create your own affirmations - even super-specific affirmations - or borrow from other people that you admire. The ThinkUp app is a great tool for finding affirmations and noting your own affirmations.
- Remember that gratitude and humility go hand in hand. It's really important to stay humble on the way up and remember that being successful doesn't make you better than other people - just as being at rock bottom doesn't make you worse than other people.

We're reaching the end of this first part of the book. But before we move onto the next part, there's one last thing you have to do. You have to learn to let go and forgive yourself. Turn the page to find out what that involves.

Chapter 4

FREEING YOURSELF THROUGH FORGIVENESS

Bill and his daughter were visiting my family for the afternoon. The barbecue was on. The sun was shining. Bill was doing his best to appear happy and relaxed but I knew him too well. There was a vague darkness underneath the surface.

By this point, Bill had done a lot of work on himself. He'd looked deep into himself, embraced gratitude and humility, and was learning to take better care of his needs. And yet, I could see he was still struggling to turn a corner. Something was holding him back, preventing him from moving forwards. I wondered if he knew what it was and was trying to hide it, or if it was a subconscious something holding him back.

THE HIDDEN WEIGHT HOLDING YOU DOWN AT ROCK BOTTOM

'So what's up?' I asked him, when we had a few minutes to ourselves.

'How'd you mean?' Bill replied.

'You've been doing so well lately, but you seem … kind of flat. Are you having a down day or is it more than that?'

Bill sighed. His attention was on his daughter, who was lazing with my daughter on a blanket at the other end of the garden. A couple of pre-teens trying to get as far away from their parents as possible, in case we cramped their style.

'I think it's more than just a down day,' Bill said. 'I've been feeling so … so angry lately. I can't shake it off, even with all the work I've been doing on myself. It's like I want to move on, but there's this weight on me, keeping me stuck here. I really, really don't want to be stuck here anymore. Worse, I'm worried I'll end up going backwards. Undoing all the hard work I've done so far.'

'What are you angry about?' I asked.

He looked at me like it was the most obvious answer in the world. 'Are you kidding?'

'No,' I said. 'Tell me. Put it into words. What are you so angry about?'

'Her,' he said, gesturing towards his daughter. 'How could she leave Callie?'

'Well,' I said carefully, 'she didn't leave Callie, as such. You share custody. She left the marriage.'

'Alright then, I'm angry that she broke up our family. How can she not see the damage it's doing?'

'Callie seems to be coping pretty well, considering,' I reassured him. 'It's you I'm worried about. You've got to get out of this headspace or you'll never be able to move on. You don't want to be one of those people who are stuck holding onto something that happened to them decades ago. You know the kinds of people. They wear their hurt like a badge of honour. It defines them.'

'I can't help how I feel,' Bill said, defensively.

'With respect,' I said. 'I think your therapist would contradict you on that point. You can help how you feel. You're in control. You can choose to forgive her.'

LEARNING TO FORGIVE THOSE WHO HAVE HURT YOU

Bill laughed. 'Forgive her? You're supposed to be on my side!'

'I am on your side,' I said. 'That's exactly why I think you should forgive her. All the time you're holding onto this negativity and pain, you'll never be able to fully heal. Try to forgive her. I mean, what have you got to lose?'

'Sorry, I just can't see it happening,' he replied. 'I don't think I'll ever forgive her for this. She walked out on our family. That's a pretty big thing to forgive someone for.'

'It is. But I read this story the other day about a woman who forgave the man who murdered her sister. The whole family forgave him, even though he'd taken away someone so precious to them. That's the ultimate forgiveness. If they can forgive something so devastating–'

'–Well, they're better people than me.' Bill cut me off and shrugged.

'It's not about being a good person or a bad person. It's about doing what you need to do to move on.'

'So you'd forgive someone who murdered your child, would you?'

I nodded, 'For my own sake, yes. I'd at least try to.'

'And what if they weren't even sorry for it?' Bill challenged me.

'Well,' I sighed. 'Sometimes you have to learn to forgive not because the other person deserves your forgiveness, but because *you* deserve it. Because you deserve peace.'

Bill thought about that for a moment.

HURT PEOPLE HURT PEOPLE

'Did I ever tell you about my friend from uni?' I asked Bill. 'The one whose husband turned out to be a right narcissist?'

Bill shook his head. 'I don't think so.'

'It all started so well. He was super-attentive and loving. Showered her with affection and gifts. She thought she'd met the one. It wasn't long before they were engaged, then married and a baby followed quickly after that. It was a whirlwind. But as soon as she was locked in, so to speak, as soon as that ring was on her finger, he started to show his true colours. Look at the checklist for domestic abuse and this guy was ticking most of the boxes, short of actually beating her up.'

'Ugh,' Bill made a disgusted sound.

'Exactly. There was the emotional abuse. He was controlling with money, literally giving her pocket money to live on. He was insanely jealous to the point where she would turn down social invites. She knew if she went on a girls' night out, she'd have to endure days of sulking. He gradually alienated her from her friends until she had no friends left of her own. Her friends were "their" friends. He moved her to a new town, away from her family. And when she did see her family, she would have to bend over backwards to keep him happy. One time they went on a family holiday with her parents and he refused to sit with the parents at the beach. He insisted that she and the baby sit with him further up the beach, away from her parents. Can you imagine that? And when she finally left, that's when he got *really* nasty. He called the police on her saying she'd hit him, when she hadn't. He tried to go for full custody saying she was an unfit mother. He destroyed her possessions. He used the baby like a weapon. He sent threatening text after threatening text. Even threatening suicide.'

'And this is a story about forgiveness?' Bill asked. 'Surely you can't forgive someone like that. Because people like that never change. If she's co-parenting with him, she must constantly have to deal with his nonsense.'

'She does,' I said. 'But she found a way to forgive him. I'm not saying it's easy. She probably has to forgive him over and over again as he continues to be a total narcissist. But she told me that she realised something really important...'

'Go on,' Bill said.

'She realised that he wasn't a happy person. He behaved the way he did because underneath the flashy persona, he was an insecure, unhappy person. And because his own father was a narcissist. He didn't have a happy upbringing. To some extent he was programmed to be the way he was.'

'Ah,' Bill said.

'That doesn't excuse him, obviously,' I said. 'Loads of people have terrible role models or bad upbringings, but they turn it around and work to be better. He wasn't able to do that. My point is, my friend finally came to realise that she couldn't change her ex. Only he could change his behaviour. But she could choose to focus on her own happiness and her own future. And to do that, she had to let go of how he'd treated her. If she held onto those negative feelings, it would be like he was still controlling her from afar.'

I continued, 'What she said really inspired me. It spurred me on to be better at forgiving people. Like with my mum. For a while I was angry at her for not seeking help for her depression. Things could have been so much better for her, and for our relationship. But I took a leaf out of my friend's book and tried to let go of those feelings. I decided to focus on my own happiness and actions, not the things my mum did or didn't do. She did her best, based on the tools she had available to her and the sum of her own experiences. Anyway, I'm not saying your wife did what she did because of her upbringing or anything. Just that, well, she did what she did. You don't have to like it. You don't have to agree with it. But like my friend, you can still forgive her.'

'So you think this is what's holding me back?' Bill asked.

'Given everything else you've been doing so far, yes. I think if you can find forgiveness, you'll begin to turn that corner.'

LEARNING TO FORGIVE YOURSELF AS WELL

The root cause of Bill's funk was clear. He'd embraced gratitude and humility and self-care. He'd faced up to his grief and loss. But he had not embraced forgiveness. And as Bill would later tell me, it turned out that the hurt from his broken marriage was bringing up all sorts of grievances from the past. A friend who had stabbed Bill in the back. The unscrupulous business partners who'd led to his startup folding years earlier. Bill was even angry at his father for dying.

Worse, he was angry at himself. For trusting unreliable business partners. For not being a better husband. And he was angry at himself for feeling so stuck. Why couldn't he just move on like a 'normal' person?

On the surface, Bill looked like your average calm and capable bloke – but underneath he was carrying around so much unresolved anger and negativity.

After our chat, I sent him a book called *The Gift of Forgiveness,* with stories about how other people had found forgiveness. He called me up a few days later, once he'd finished reading it.

'There was the saddest story in there about this woman whose son was one of the Columbine school shooters,' Bill said. 'Heart-wrenching.'

'And she learned to forgive her son?' I asked.

'Well that, and forgive herself. She blamed herself for not being a better parent, or not recognising red flags about his mental health. But she had to learn to forgive herself for the things she didn't notice or just didn't know. Because we can't fully know what's going on inside other people's heads.'

'Blimey, that can't have been easy.'

'Of course not,' Bill said. 'And it's an ongoing process. It made me think, though. You were right. I need to forgive. Not just my wife, but all the other resentments I've been holding onto. And I need to forgive myself. If this mother can do it, I can. It's like you said, I deserve peace. That, if nothing else, is a reason to forgive.'

'I think that's great,' I said. 'So how are you going to become this all-forgiving person?'

'Good question,' Bill laughed. 'It's something I've been talking to my therapist about. She said the first step is to really understand what forgiveness is. It's not about making excuses or forgetting about what's happened. It's just a conscious decision to release those feelings of anger and resentment, towards others and myself. It's got nothing to do with whether they deserve it or not. It's just about letting go of my negative feelings.'

'Sounds smart.'

'She also said it's not necessarily a one-and-done thing. I mean, I can consciously choose to release those feelings, but I may have to keep working at it. Like, if I'm tempted to say something bad about my ex-wife – or put myself down for something I did – I need to catch myself in that process. It's a continual practice.'

I couldn't help but smile. 'Well, now I know you're going to ace this.'

'How so?' Bill asked.

'Look at what you've been doing with gratitude and making time for yourself. You've made an ongoing commitment to therapy and working on your mental health. You can do this. Even if it's hard work sometimes, you've got this.'

'Thanks, mate,' Bill said. 'I hope so.'

'I think you're going to look back and realise this was a key moment. This was when you were truly ready to start building that better life you've been talking about.'

On the other end of the phone, Bill said, 'I have to admit, though, it's scary.'

FREEING YOURSELF FROM FEAR

'How do you mean?' I asked.

'Well,' Bill said. 'There's a weird kind of comfort in staying angry at people, isn't there? It's like a shield. Like, I won't let anyone else hurt me again because I've got this shield up. Forgiveness feels a bit like letting my defences down again. I mean, I know it's actually a really strong thing to do, but a lot of people think forgiveness is weak and I kind of see their point. What if you forgive someone and then the same thing happens again?'

'So staying angry and resentful feels safer than moving on?'

'Kind of,' Bill admitted. 'I know that's messed up. But I think that's perhaps what's been holding me back. I want to let go of negative feelings, but I don't want to get hurt again.'

I thought for a moment. 'You remember when your business failed and how that felt?'

'Yes...' Bill said, as though he had no idea where I was going with this.

'Me too!' I said. 'When one of my businesses failed, it stung like hell. But I wasn't going to let it hold me back from trying other things. Successful people aren't successful because they never get knocked down. Just like happy people aren't happy because they never experience anything bad. Happy people are happy because they don't let the bad experiences define them. Likewise, successful people are successful because they know that failure doesn't define them - it's just another stepping stone on the journey. You nearly went broke when your business went under, but look at you now: you're a global VP in a hugely successful business.'

'Well, it's not my business,' Bill said.

'No, but you found a new version of success. You weren't defined by your business failing. You moved on. You rebuilt.'

'I don't get what this has to do with forgiveness.'

I clarified. 'You're afraid that forgiving might open you up to future hurt, right? That you might have another relationship break down like this one, or someone else might screw you over. Right?'

'Right,' Bill agreed.

'Deep down, it's just fear of failure. Fear of things going wrong. Trouble is, that fear can close you off from accepting new opportunities - whether it's a new relationship, a new job, or whatever else comes your way. I see it so many times with the people I mentor, people who desperately want to become property developers and build their own wealth. These are smart people, who may be very successful in other parts of their life, but they fear making the leap because they worry it'll all go wrong. That kind of fear is so limiting. It stops you fulfilling your potential.'

'I see,' Bill said.

'Things went wrong before and you got through it. Your marriage broke down and you're getting through it. You can't go through life avoiding other potential failures or you'll avoid all the things that could go right. It's time to let go of all that negative stuff. The resentment and anger. And the fear.'

HOW TO PUT ALL THIS INTO PRACTICE

Whatever your rock bottom looks like - whether it's a financial low, an emotional low, or something else entirely - forgiveness can be the missing piece of the puzzle. Because when you hold onto negative feelings about others (and even yourself), it will stop you moving forwards.

Forgiveness is a continual process. It's something you'll have to practise and get better at over time. And you'll have to stay alert to feelings of anger and resentment when they creep in.

And listen, I know that anger can occasionally be a positive motivator. If someone tells you that you can't do something and that makes you angry, the anger might spur you on to prove that person wrong. The problem is when you're holding onto anger about things that you simply cannot change. You don't have to be happy about the things that have happened to you, but you can choose to let go of the anger.

The tools you'll learn throughout this book will help you let go of negative emotions, let go of the past and focus on the future (and the present). But in this chapter, we'll explore some practical tips that focus specifically on forgiveness.

As Bill's therapist told him, the first step is to understand what forgiveness is and isn't:

- Forgiveness is simply letting go of negative feelings towards yourself or another person.
- It's got nothing to do with whether someone deserves your forgiveness. We can forgive because *we* deserve it - because we deserve to find peace and to focus on the future.
- It doesn't mean you're happy about what has happened to you or that you excuse the other person's behaviour (or your own for that matter). Forgiveness doesn't mean you pretend it never happened. It just means you're ready to move on.
- Forgiveness is strength, not weakness.

Interestingly, forgiveness has been proven to have very real physical and mental benefits. Forgiveness is associated with lower levels of anxiety, depression and anger, as well as higher self-esteem. Isn't that amazing?

ACKNOWLEDGE THE HURT AND ANGER

When you don't forgive, you hold onto anger and negativity – and, as a result, the main person who suffers is you. Negative feelings do not serve you. In fact, they can lead to all sorts of harmful behaviours, like drinking too much to mask the emotional pain, or hurting others you love. They can even lead to health issues, such as stress, anxiety, depression and insomnia.

This is why it's so important to acknowledge the pain you feel and *why* you feel that way. Who is it that hurt you? Who, exactly, do you need to forgive?

It may sound obvious, but this step is easily brushed aside. Bill, for example, was angry at his wife, and that in turn brought up all sorts of resentments that he hadn't properly acknowledged. Bill still hadn't forgiven the business partners who'd let him down years ago. He hadn't worked through the feelings surrounding his father's death. And when his wife left, all that submerged pain came bubbling to the surface.

So acknowledge the pain you feel in order to understand who needs forgiveness. (And don't forget, that person could be you.)

TRY TO FIND EMPATHY

One way to forgive someone else is to put yourself in their shoes. Sue Klebold, the mother of one of the Columbine shooters, has spoken openly about how empathy and forgiveness go hand in hand for her. To put herself in her son's shoes, she went on a learning journey and researched brain health. Ultimately, she began to understand that her son, Dylan, didn't make his decision in the same way that you or I would make a decision. His brain was working differently. Understanding that allowed her to forgive him, and herself.

In a similar way, my friend learned to forgive her narcissistic ex by examining his life - his upbringing, the unhappiness inside him, his insecurities.

Try to remember that we all carry (or have carried) hurt inside ourselves. And some people take this out on others. As the saying goes, hurt people hurt people. This doesn't mean that everyone has free rein to be horrible to each other. Nor does it mean that you should let people treat you poorly. You should absolutely set and maintain boundaries around how you expect to be treated.

But to release the anger about what has already been, it may help to remember that most people are just doing the best that they know how, given their circumstances and life experience.

Now, I personally don't believe that people should be victims of their upbringing or struggles. Everyone has the ability to change their behaviour, if they choose. It may require a lot of work and perhaps professional help, but anyone can change. The fact that my friend's ex chooses not to change is up to him. But she can still forgive and let go of her own hurt and anger.

If you really struggle to empathise with someone who has caused you pain, try to imagine them as an innocent baby - when they were a clean slate, before they learned their behaviours or experienced their own struggles.

FORGIVE YOURSELF

The person you need to forgive could be you. Because like others, you've made decisions and acted in ways that you perhaps aren't proud of. But have you noticed that we tend to be harder on ourselves than we are on others? When your child makes a mistake, for example, I bet you react with more understanding than you do when you make a mistake yourself.

Stop blaming yourself. Stop blaming yourself for the things that aren't your fault. And stop blaming yourself for the things that are your fault. Because, just like most other people on this planet, you're generally doing the best you can do with the tools that are currently available to you. Let go of the blame and negative feelings about yourself, to make space for more positive feelings.

The great thing is, you can always learn new tools to help you change (in those areas where you want to change). You can learn to love and take care of yourself. You can set and achieve exciting goals for yourself. You can shift your mindset through tools like visualisation and gratitude. You can work with a life coach, as I did. Or a therapist, as Bill did. But it's difficult to make those changes if you don't forgive yourself first.

Depending on your circumstances, this step might also involve asking for forgiveness from the people you've harmed.

REMEMBER, IT'S A PROCESS

Forgiveness is a decision, but it's also a process. If you struggle with that process, don't be too hard on yourself. It can be bloody hard to forgive. Especially if, like my friend, the person you forgive continues to try and cause you harm.

Where possible, it's great to forgive quickly, so that you can move on and focus on what's next. But sometimes forgiveness takes time. And that's okay too. Be patient with yourself.

When you trip up - for example, when you think something horrible about a person you're trying to forgive - cut yourself some slack.

Acknowledge how you feel and gently remind yourself why you want to forgive that person (i.e. because you deserve to forgive).

You can also try practising forgiveness in little ways on a regular basis. When someone carves you up in traffic, forgive them and let go of the temptation to wish herpes on them! When someone gives you terrible service in a café or shop, use that as an opportunity to practise empathy. They may be having a much worse day than you.

And if you can, try to surround yourself with people who are also forgiving. It can be hard to focus on positivity when the people around you dwell in negativity and anger. Try to spend more time with people who lift you up, rather than keeping you weighed down at rock bottom.

FOCUS ON BEING THE BEST YOU CAN BE

Another tip is to simply concentrate on yourself. Focus on being the best possible version of you. Because, at the end of the day, forgiveness is about you moving on. So stay laser-focused on what *you* want and how *you* want to live your life. Go after those things with a passion, without looking back at the events and people that have caused you harm.

In fact, I try to live by this rule in all aspects of life, not just forgiveness. In business, for example, I don't look at what my competitors are doing. I'm never out to one-up other property developers. I'm only ever looking at my business, my goals and my plan. If I were to focus on being one step ahead of a certain competitor, then yes, I may end up slightly better than that competitor. But that's not necessarily the best I can possibly be. Far better to focus only on doing my best, and building the business I want to lead.

I find this is a good way to stay positive and direct my energy in a more constructive way.

LET GO OF FEAR

And finally, don't be afraid of failing or getting hurt in future. In fact, get comfortable with the fact that things will not always go to plan.

Will others cause you pain in future? Almost certainly. Will you be imperfect yourself? Definitely. Should that stop you letting go of the past and striving for a better future? Hell no.

Rock bottom can be a frightening place. I know, I've been there. To move beyond rock bottom, you have to let go of that fear and focus on the things that could go right, not the things that may go wrong. Feel the fear and do it anyway? That sounds about right. But we'll talk more about this concept in Chapter 8.

LESSONS FROM ROCK BOTTOM

- When you hold onto negativity, anger and pain, it can stop you from fully healing and moving forwards. Forgiveness allows you to let go of pain and negative emotions.
- Forgiveness has nothing to do with whether another person deserves your forgiveness or not. *You* deserve to forgive. You deserve to find peace.
- Forgiveness doesn't mean you're happy about what has happened to you or that you excuse someone else's behaviour. Forgiveness doesn't mean you pretend it never happened. It just means you want to move on.
- Forgiveness can deliver very real physical and mental benefits, such as lower levels of anxiety, depression and anger, and higher self-esteem.
- Empathy is a good path to forgiveness. Try to remember that we all experience pain and struggles. And we are all, generally, doing our best with the tools available to us.
- Forgive yourself, too. Let go of self-blame and negative feelings about yourself. Make space for more positive feelings.

- Forgiveness is a decision, but it's also a process. As such, it may take time, and you may need to continually work at it. Try to catch yourself when negative thoughts surface and turn it into a moment of forgiveness. But at the same time, don't be too hard on yourself.
- Stop focusing on what other people do and say, and instead concentrate on your own self. Forgiveness isn't about anyone but you. So stay laser-focused on what *you* want and how *you* want to live your life.
- And finally, let go of fear. Anger and resentment can feel like a shield that protects you from future hurt, but that's not the case. (If anything these negative emotions only cause you more damage.) Let go of the fear that things may go wrong again. That you may fail. That you may get hurt. Focus on what you want not what you don't want.

You probably picked up this book because you wanted to know how to move beyond rock bottom. And yet our friend Bill hasn't made huge strides forward yet, has he? Or perhaps it's more accurate to say Bill has been taking the odd step forward and the odd step back and the odd step sideways. That's okay. Most people don't bounce back from rock bottom immediately. Like Bill, you may need time to build your strength and resilience through things like gratitude, self-care and forgiveness. That's what this part of the book has been about.

In the next part, we'll begin to move forwards. Because finding forgiveness was a critical turning point for Bill. This was when he truly began to build the life he wanted for himself and his daughter. But we'll learn more about Bill's journey in the next couple of parts...

Part II:
Preparing For The Climb

LAYING THE GROUNDWORK FOR YOUR FUTURE LIFE

'Rock bottom became the solid foundation in which I rebuilt my life.'

–J K ROWLING

Chapter 5

FINDING YOUR WHY

'I don't get it,' I said to Bill. 'Why am I looking at a piece of blank paper?'

Bill had asked me to pop over for a coffee, saying that he needed to borrow my brain. I was intrigued. And confused. I had no idea why he had just slid an empty notebook across the kitchen table.

'Exactly!' Bill said. 'It's blank. That's *supposed* to be a list of goals for my life.'

'Ah,' I said. 'Having trouble, are you?'

'That's why you're here,' Bill nodded. 'I want to rebuild my life the way you rebuilt yours. Well, not exactly the same, obviously. But I want you to tell me how you went from losing nearly everything to what you've got now - financial freedom, successful businesses, happy relationship, exciting plans for the future... How'd you get started towards all that? What first steps did you plan out?'

'Okay,' I exhaled. 'That's a big question. But first, let me ask you this: what have you done so far to come up with your goals?'

'Mostly just staring at this empty notebook,' Bill laughed. 'I mean, I have a vague dream in my head - me and Callie, the two of us happy and well. Me free of the past, feeling better than I have in years. Feeling satisfied with my life. But when I try to turn that into an action plan ... nothing. My mind goes blank. Nothing flows out. I've been trying for the last week. I keep coming back to this notebook, sitting here with my pen in my hand, waiting for inspiration to strike. And each time, nothing. It's like I've got the goal-setting equivalent of writer's block.'

'I hear you,' I said. I had an inkling of where Bill might be going wrong.

He continued. 'I mean, I'm in my late forties. I thought I'd have it all figured out by now. For a while I thought I did have it all figured out - you know, the whole marriage and kids thing. But evidently not. I still don't know where my life is going. You have to help me!' he pleaded. 'Before this drives me insane.'

'Well, don't panic,' I laughed. 'Loads of people don't know what they want to do with their life. You're not alone. I hear people say all the time that they still don't know what they want to do. But do you know what that says to me?'

'Tell me.'

'That you haven't found your *why*. That's all. Take a step back, focus on finding your why and your goals will fall into place.'

IT ALL STARTS WITH PURPOSE

'My why?' Bill asked.

'Yeah, you know, your purpose, your passion. You're much more likely to achieve goals that stem from your passion. So what is it that drives you towards your future life?'

Bill looked blank and a bit despondent.

'I don't know,' he said. 'A year ago, I would have said my purpose was having this perfect family life. But now...'

'I think that's why you're struggling to set goals and bring those goals to life. You placed your why in another person and now that person's no longer here. You need to find your new why. And it shouldn't be another person. It should come from deep within you.'

Bill sighed. 'So I need to create some deep and meaningful purpose for myself. Like changing the world or something?'

'No, no, it doesn't have to be anything that grand. Your why is just about you. What are you passionate about?'

'Can't I just borrow your why?' Bill joked.

'Unfortunately not. You have to find your unique why, or whys. Listen, don't get overwhelmed by this. Just take some time out to think about what's important to you. Let that guide your future goals. It's pretty cool when you think about it. You have total freedom to create your own future here - that's the one good thing about rock bottom. It's a chance to reevaluate what's important to you, and what you want to focus on in future. Don't waste this opportunity. Give it some real thought.'

'Aren't you even going to tell me your why?' Bill asked.

'I will. But for now, concentrate on unearthing yours.'

I know many people struggle to set concrete goals for themselves - and a lot of the time, it's because they haven't tapped into their passion.

Like a lot of people, Bill had placed his purpose in someone else. He put his wife and child at the centre of his why. There's nothing wrong with including others as part of your why, but not to the extent that you exclude the self. If you can't make yourself important enough for your goals, how do you expect to achieve those goals?

To help identify his why, Bill turned to the Japanese concept of Ikigai, which translates as 'a reason for being'. The basic premise is to draw four overlapping circles, each representing one of the following prompt questions:

- What do you love?
- What are you good at?
- What does the world need?
- What can you be paid for?

You put your answers in each circle, and where the circles overlap you find your Passion, Vocation, Profession and Mission (depending on which circle overlaps with which - it helps to Google a picture of Ikigai at this point). At the very centre of the diagram, where all four circles meet, there is your why. That's the idea, anyway. But it wasn't exactly going to plan for Bill.

AVOIDING THE LURE OF EXTERNAL WHYS

When I next saw Bill, his attempt at Ikigai looked like this:

- Under 'What do you love?' he'd written: my daughter, friends, family, seeing people smile.
- Under 'What are you good at?' he'd written: talking to people, cooking, being a dad.
- Under 'What does the world need?' he'd written: peace, kindness, tolerance.
- And under 'What can you be paid for?' he'd written: leadership.

And at the centre, where his why was supposed to be, there sat a big, fat question mark.

'This method doesn't work,' Bill said.

Still looking at the diagram, I said, 'Well, if I may, there's something pretty big missing from here.'

'What?' Bill asked. 'I've done all four circles. What's missing?'

'Look hard,' I prompted.

Bill studied his diagram and then finally said, 'Me.'

'Yes!' I said. 'We need to get more Bill in here. Look, let's start with what do you love? Yes, of course you love your child, friends, etc. but those are all external to you. Take your daughter, for example. Thinking selfishly, what is it about having children that truly touches you? Thinking purely from *your* point of view...'

'I guess it's the way she makes me feel when she's happy and content. I feel amazing knowing I've helped give her the tools to be happy and content in life.'

'Right? It's a subtle distinction, but it's an important one. So let's rewrite these categories in a more selfish way.'

And we did. We started with a blank sheet of paper and redrew Bill's four circles, refocusing his answers on what *he* wanted and needed.

- For 'What do you love?' Bill answered: being nurturing, laughter, food, nature, feeling held and supported by others, belonging.
- For 'What are you good at?' we ended up reframing the question to focus more on the inner Bill. (After all, lots of people are good at things that they hate doing.) Instead I asked him, 'What feels good to you when you're doing it?' His answer: writing, being outdoors, helping others.
- We also reframed 'What does the world need' to 'What does BILL's world need?' His answer: self-satisfaction, more time for things I love, less technology.
- And finally, for 'What can you be paid for?' I encouraged Bill to think not just about money, but how it feels to be rewarded in other ways. His answer came out of the blue and surprised even himself: helping others get through dark times.

And at the centre of it all, where the circles overlapped, Bill wrote three things:

- Freedom
- A sense of community
- Turning my experience into a positive for others

After all the procrastinating and false starts, Bill had found his whys. His unique purpose.

ASSESSING YOUR LIFE THROUGH THE LENS OF YOUR WHYS

'This is amazing,' I said to Bill. 'You've nailed it.'

Bill was beaming. 'It feels like I've cracked it. This feels right.'

'So now the tough question: What about your life as it stands right now isn't fulfilling your whys?'

Bill answered instantly, 'My job.'

'Go on...' I encouraged him.

After a few seconds' thought, Bill said, 'I certainly don't hate what I do now. It pays well. I love my team and the clients I get to work with. But I'd be lying if I said I was passionate about it. You know I fell into the corporate world when my business folded – and don't get me wrong, I was so grateful to fall on my feet so quickly – but I never imagined I'd still be doing it nearly 20 years later. When I think about doing this for the next 20 years ... pfff.'

'You want to be your own boss again?' I asked.

'I guess so. I always assumed I would one day, but hadn't thought about it in so long. But yeah, I loved the freedom of running my own business. Work felt like play back then. If I could achieve that again, that feeling that I'm barely even *working*, that would be life-changing.'

'Sounds like you're in a great place to start creating some goals, eh?' I said, smiling.

Bill sat back in his chair, slightly stunned. 'It's funny. These past few months I've been so focused on the end of my marriage, it hadn't occurred to me to consider a career change. I've been so focused on trying to picture a happy life for me and Callie.'

'But having a career that you're passionate about is a key element of success and happiness, don't you think? Family and friends, human connections, they're all vital. But so is that feeling of satisfaction within yourself. The work you do feeds into that feeling. And it feeds into the happiness you feel in other areas. I know it does for me.'

'I guess I forgot that for a while,' Bill said. 'So come on, you've got inside my head. Fancy sharing your whys?'

HOW I FOUND MY PASSION

Here's what I told Bill...

I didn't know my why for a long time. I'd always been entrepreneurial, was always starting funny little businesses when I was a schoolboy - I even sold the koi carp out of the family fish pond! But I never connected that entrepreneurial passion to what I wanted to do for the rest of my life.

Because I'd been conditioned, by my parents and society, to believe that I should grow up, go to university, get a well-paying job, and settle into it for the next forty years.

So, like a good boy, I went to uni, took a sidestep from my original studies (engineering) into studying IT, and ended up getting a lucrative IT job. IT was booming at the time (I mean, when isn't it?) and I was earning a great salary for my age. But I wasn't happy. I wasn't connecting to my passion.

To help cover the mortgage as a single guy living in the expensive south of England, I rented out a spare room in my house to one of my friends. I loved it. I was having a great time living with my mate *and* earning extra cash for the privilege. Why isn't everyone doing this, I wondered? Then I rented out the second spare room to another tenant and was overnight earning enough in rental income to cover my mortgage each month.

Then I converted the garage into another rental bedroom, and the income from that room was my first taste of passive income. Roughly £500 a month in rental income leftover after paying my mortgage. And for doing ... what? Just renting out rooms that would otherwise accumulate junk and guitars! Seriously, why wasn't everyone doing this?

I was hooked on passive income and property. I was hooked on the idea of being my own boss, investing in property, and achieving my own financial freedom - instead of working to make my bosses rich (which is all I was doing in my previous career).

That was my original why. And it may seem like it landed in my lap without me having to do anything. But the truth is I made space for that passion to reveal itself, by doing more of the things that felt good to me.

From there, I quit my job and began to build a small portfolio of rental properties, and then started to dip my toe into property development. And that's about when the financial crisis of 2008 hit, at which point I lost almost everything I'd worked so hard to build. That was when I ended up living in that crappy flat in Dover, desperate to rebuild my finances, my career and my life. I was at rock bottom. But I knew my steadfast connection to my passion would help me get back everything I'd lost, and more.

YOUR WHYS AREN'T SET IN STONE

As I've travelled on this amazing journey from my own rock bottom to where I am today, owning a multi-million-pound property portfolio, I've connected with other whys along the way.

Underneath it all, being my own boss, keeping out of the rat race, and building financial freedom are still there at the core. But there are new whys, like mentoring and teaching others. This has become an increasingly pressing why over the last few years. I've learned a lot from my ups and downs in property and running my own businesses - and now I'm at the point where I can dedicate time to passing that knowledge onto others. I do this through mentorship programmes, running courses for budding property developers, and writing books like this. I'm not writing this book for you. Well, I am, obviously, but I'm mostly writing it because I LOVE it.

Education has become a major passion for me. And as such, that shapes a lot of my goals.

And yes, some of my whys and passions are external. The grownup in me wants my kids to be proud of me, and to build a legacy for them. Meanwhile, the little boy in me still wants my parents to be proud of me.

But I don't live by external whys at the expensive of my internal whys. That's a dangerous path. Because those external whys can disappear without warning.

As an unhappy coincidence, Bill and I had both lost a parent in the past year. My dad died a few months before I started writing this book, and at the time of writing, my mum is seriously ill in hospital. Recently, after I'd had a fantastic weekend running a property course, it occurred to me that I couldn't call either of them up to tell them about my success. Dad was gone and Mum was, at that point, lying unconscious and fighting for her life in a hospital bed. That moment hit hard and I felt more alone than I had in a long time. But that moment would have been a hell of a lot harder and darker if I didn't have other whys.

HOW TO FIND YOUR WHY

We'll talk about setting clear goals in the next chapter. But for now, your job is to uncover your why (or whys). What are you passionate about? What is your purpose in life? What drives you to rebuild from rock bottom and create the life of your dreams?

Whatever goals you set for yourself – and don't get hung up on specific goals yet – the biggest tip I can give you is to connect your goals to your passion. Your passion could be anything. Your passion could be a specific activity, like a hobby that you decide to turn into a job. It could simply be an aspirational feeling – like Bill wanting to feel free and create a sense of community.

Bottom line, goals stick better when they connect to your why.

Trouble is, when you're at rock bottom, you may not be feeling particularly inspired. You may have lost touch with the things that make you tick. That was certainly the case for Bill. He turned to the Ikigai method, and tools like that are definitely a great place to start – so long as you use them correctly and stay focused on your internal whys, instead of getting caught up in external whys.

I found that my whys evolved and grew over time, and you'll probably find the same thing. That's great. But underneath it all, especially when you're starting the journey from rock bottom, it's really important to start with your selfish whys, before progressing to wider purposes and passions.

So like Bill, use tools like Ikigai, but use them as a way to uncover what YOU want.

TIPS FOR IDENTIFYING YOUR WHY

Here are some other powerful ways to identify your why and connect with your passion:

- My biggest tip is to **make time for yourself**. I firmly believe that one of the reasons Bill couldn't connect with his why was because he struggled to make time for his own needs. The sad truth is, too many people just don't make time to think about what they really want from life. If you're the same, try to carve out moments of peace away from the stresses of life, kids, work, etc. This could be taking a walk, having a mindful moment, gardening, riding a bike, or whatever. Just make time for yourself.

- It's also important to **have hobbies**. I love what I do for a living, but I love my hobbies even more. Because hobbies are mindful. Fishing, playing guitar, camping with the kids ... these all help me find calm and connect with my inner self. They also allow me to have fun. And time for fun activities, things that make you feel good, is so important. Especially when you're feeling uninspired. You may even find that your hobby leads to a career, as it did for Peter Jones from Dragon's Den, who liked computers so much his first business was building and selling computers. Another of his businesses was a cocktail bar inspired by the Tom Cruise movie *Cocktail*. You may not end up a millionaire by turning your hobby into a business, but at least you'll be connecting to your passion.
- And if you don't have any hobbies? Well then, **think back to your childhood hobbies**. What did you love doing when you were a child? Could that translate into a passion (or even a career) for the adult you? If you were on the school cricket team, for example, join the local cricket team or coach a youth team. If your idea of a good time was helping Grandad at the allotment, get an allotment. Grow. Get your fingers dirty. You get the idea.
- You might also **ask yourself, who inspires you**? And how can you do more of what they do? If a particular writer inspires you, write! Write anything – bad poetry, letters to loved ones, fan fiction, anything. If a musician inspires you, learn to play an instrument. If an activist inspires you, work out how you can devote some of your time to a cause that's important to you.
- And also, **read other people's stories of success**. I'm an avid reader, especially when it comes to biographies and autobiographies of successful people. I just love reading stories of how other people have found their purpose and built an amazing life. Maybe you could find inspiration in similar stories?

STAYING CONNECTED TO YOUR WHY

Your why should serve as a fantastic motivator on your journey from rock bottom. (We'll also talk about other ways to stay motivated in Chapter 11.)

But how can you maintain a super-strong connection to your why? How can you keep it front and centre in your mind?

One tool that I love is called the dream board. This is simply a collage of pictures and words that capture on paper what it is that you want out of life. It's a fun way to concentrate the mind and maintain focus on your passions – especially if you go to town with really beautiful, aspirational pictures. For example, for my friend Bill, his dream board might include pictures of him on a guy's trip from a few years ago (sense of community), or a beautiful mountain scene (nature), or a sun lounger in his garden (freedom), or a picture from a time when he felt happy, satisfied and in charge of his life direction.

I strongly recommend you create your own dream board to capture your passions on paper. This tool is so impactful, I even encourage my kids to have their own dream boards. But since the dream board is closely connected to setting goals, we'll talk more about it in the next chapter.

LESSONS FOR THE CLIMB

- You're much more likely to strive for a goal that connects to your passion. So before you try setting any goals for your climb from rock bottom, first connect to your why. Your passion. Your reason for wanting to build a better life.
- Rock bottom is a chance to reevaluate what's important to you, and how you want to spend your time in future. This is an incredible opportunity. So take the time to really think about your why.
- It's vital that your primary why (or whys) comes from within you. Don't place your sole purpose in another person – be selfish for a

moment and think about what makes *you* happy and brings *you* satisfaction.
- Remember, it's perfectly normal for your whys to evolve over time.
- If you're struggling to connect to your why, the Japanese concept of Ikigai or 'reason for being' may help. But again, use this as a tool to drill down to internal whys, not external.
- Most people are too busy to make time to think about what they really want from life. So make time and headspace to connect to your passion.
- Other ways to identify your why include: making time for your hobbies, looking at the people who inspire you, and reading stories of how other people have built a life that's in line with their passion.

Once you've connected to your why, you can begin to translate that into concrete goals - goals that help you create the life you desire. Which brings us to the next chapter, and the next phase of Bill's journey...

Chapter 6

SETTING YOUR GOALS (BIG AND SMALL)

An idea had begun to form in Bill's head. A vague notion at first, that had begun to crystalise into something more concrete.

'I want to start my own non-profit,' Bill explained to me. 'An organisation that works with men who find themselves at rock bottom. Because if my experience has taught me anything, it's that this can happen to anyone, at any time of life. And I feel like men maybe aren't so great at getting help when they need it.'

'So it's like a counselling thing?' I asked.

'No, not formal counselling. I was thinking more healing through nature. Camping, bushcraft, foraging, hiking, cooking outdoors, that sort of thing. I thought I could lead the trips. I used to be quite an outdoorsman when I was younger.'

'Brilliant. Scouts, but for grownups, right?'

'Kind of,' Bill laughed. 'Just something that helps men at rock bottom get away from their situation, whatever it may be, and find community with other men who are also struggling. All free of course, for men who need it. Local at first. But who knows, maybe one day it could grow to become a national organisation.'

'I love it,' I said to Bill.

'Really?'

'Absolutely. I know the difference a few hours of fishing makes to my mood. The power of being outdoors is huge. And building that sense of community at the same time? Seriously, I love it.'

'Yeah, I'm excited,' Bill said. 'And it feels good to feel excited about something again. But also, if I'm honest, I'm a bit daunted by it all. I've run a business before, but never a charity. There would be a lot of steps to get this off the ground. Getting funding for starters. I wouldn't know where to start. I don't know, maybe I'm not the best person to do this.'

'Of course you are!' I reassured him. 'You know the drill here: it's a case of turning your dream into specific goals, and then breaking those goals down into manageable smaller goals.'

'I know all that, up here,' Bill tapped the side of his head. 'But it still feels like a lot for where I'm at right now. I mean, two months ago, just waking up and getting out of bed felt like a big effort. Brushing my teeth, getting dressed, making the bed ... all of that everyday stuff, stuff I used to do on autopilot, suddenly felt like running a marathon.'

'You've come a long way since then,' I said.

'I know,' Bill nodded. 'But I'm still not sleeping that well.'

'Still? I had no idea.'

'Yeah,' Bill sighed. 'I feel like I've got some more work to do to build my inner strength, you know? I think that's where I want to focus my energy for now.'

GOALS DON'T HAVE TO BE BIG

'That's okay,' I said. 'You can still practise setting and achieving goals, even if it's not some big huge life goal like starting your own non-profit.'

'Not sure I follow.'

'Think about it, how did you get into the habit of doing gratitude every day?'

Bill looked confused for a moment. 'Well, it was just little things really. I decided to say thank you every morning when I woke up, just to start my day with some positivity. I even kept a post-it note next to my bed with "SAY THANK YOU" written on it in big letters. And then after that I list my three things to be grateful for.'

'Those were mini-goals you set for yourself. Say thank you every morning. List three things to be grateful for. They're goals. You maybe didn't see them as goals at the time, but that's what they are.'

'Hmm,' Bill said. 'I suppose they are.'

'And exercise?' I asked. 'How did you get back into your exercise routine?'

This was something I know Bill had struggled with in the aftermath of the split. But he'd been easing back into his usual workout routine for the last few weeks.

'Well, that wasn't so easy,' Bill said. 'It wasn't just a case of *deciding* to exercise. I've been exhausted and completely lacking in any motivation.'

He thought for a moment then continued, 'Actually, one thing I started doing was laying out my gym clothes the night before. It just took away that moment's decision in the morning. That moment where I'd decide whether to put on my gym clothes and go to the gym, or put on normal clothes and not bother. The gym clothes were already there. I'd put them on without thinking and go do a workout, even if it was just a short one.'

'And are you still having to lay out your workout clothes every night, and look at your post-it note every morning?'

'Huh, not so much,' Bill replied. 'I'm pretty much in the habit of exercising regularly again, and the gratitude thing has become second nature. I don't need to be prompted to do it anymore.'

'So you were setting these mini-goals every day. And they became habits that built up to you achieving the things you wanted: being more grateful, being more positive, and looking after yourself better.'

'I guess,' Bill said. 'I never thought of it that way.'

'So why don't you do the same thing with your sleep? Set yourself a series of mini-goals that add up to you getting a better night's rest.'

'You want me to set sleeping as a goal?' Bill looked at me like I was crazy. 'If only it were that easy.'

'Why not? Just look for those little practical things you can do. Like ... well, what is it that happens when you go to bed? Do you have trouble dropping off or are you waking up in the middle of the night?'

'Sometimes both,' Bill admitted. 'But it's the getting to sleep that's the big issue. When I go to bed, my brain just becomes super-active and full of thoughts. Things I'm worried about. Things that have happened. Things I said 20 years ago! I lie there for hours tossing and turning and getting increasingly frustrated that I'm going to be knackered again in the morning.'

'So you need to make a list of things that will help calm your brain in the evening. Starting with knocking off that stuff,' I nodded at Bill's 5pm cup of coffee.

Bill grimaced. 'I knew you were going to say that.'

SMALL GOALS ADD UP

When I next checked in with Bill, his sleep was improving. It still wasn't perfect, but it was getting much better.

'So what are you doing differently?' I asked him.

'Well, like you said, I listed a series of mini-goals that would contribute to better sleep. So I made a deal with myself no caffeine after midday. No alcohol too close to bed. No screen time before bed or in the bedroom. I joined the library so I have a small stack of books to read next to my bed, instead of scrolling on my phone. Oh, and I've started doing my gratitude list at night. When I get into bed, I write down three things I'm grateful for from the day, and that makes me feel a little more ... in the moment, I guess. And it helps that each step is so small.'

'So it feels easy to keep it going every day,' I agreed.

'Yeah, especially now I'm starting to see the benefits. It's almost like a snowball effect. Just the process of striving for and achieving these little goals - even though they may seem insignificant to someone else - makes me feel good and keeps driving me forward.'

I nodded. 'If you want to change the world, make your bed.'

'Huh?' Bill said.

'I saw this speech by an American speaker and that's basically what he was saying. If you make your bed in the morning, you've already achieved one thing that day. You'll feel a small sense of achievement, and that will encourage you to do another task, and so on and so on...'

'Makes sense,' Bill said.

'It's funny,' I said. 'After we talked last time, I realised I set mini-goals for myself most days.'

'Oh yeah?' Bill asked.

'Definitely. I realised I do it as part of my affirmations. You know I have my general affirmations like "I am enough." Affirmations that lift me up and make me feel more positive. But I also make up specific affirmations like, "Today I will write a chapter of my book." Or "Today I will learn about that new social media platform." These aren't big life goals that I want to put on my dream board or build into my business strategy, but they still matter to me. So I say them out loud as an affirmation, and it sets my intention.'

'Maybe I'll give that a try,' Bill said. 'I could use it as a way to ease into my business idea.'

'Yes!' I said.

'Today I'm going to research how to register a non-profit. That sort of thing...'

'Great idea to do it that way. You keep it manageable, and each little achievement spurs you on to the next.'

HOW TO SET YOUR GOALS? START SMALL

Deep down, we all know how to set and achieve goals. You specify what you want to achieve, you break it down into a series of steps, and you methodically work through those steps, gradually getting closer to your end goal. But when you're at rock bottom, goal-setting can feel incredibly overwhelming and intimidating.

Perhaps it's because we tend to think that a goal must be a big-ticket item, something life-changing like becoming a millionaire or buying your dream home. And it's great to set big, exciting goals for yourself like that. After all, no one else is going to do it for you. But the reality is that big goals need to be broken down into a series of small goals. You don't just go out there and become a millionaire overnight. You may have to retrain, learn about investment techniques, build your professional network, and a whole host of other tasks along the way.

My point is, the big goals are important, but if you want to achieve the big things in life, you'd better get good at achieving the smaller things in life.

In this way, setting goals isn't just a practical process – it requires a shift in mindset. You have to learn to seek mini-wins in the normal, everyday things. Turn the mundane into a victory. Turn chores into an opportunity to pat yourself on the back. And we really are talking about little things, like making your bed in the morning, remembering to say thank you for the good things in life, getting out for a walk, and cooking something nourishing for yourself.

These small goals may not seem very important when you're desperate to scramble away from rock bottom. But they add up. Each goal you achieve, each win provides a burst of positive energy that fuels you for the next mini-goal. It builds confidence.

Whereas, if you were to *only* set big goals for yourself – huge wins like starting a new career, or getting out of debt, or regaining your health after a serious illness – you could run out of steam before you reach your destination, because you're not getting those confidence-boosting victories along the way.

Look for the little wins, then, while you strive for the huge wins.

SMALL GOALS BECOME GOOD HABITS

When you think about it, these little wins or mini-goals could also be described as good habits. In fact, goal-setting can be a great way to turn bad habits into good habits. Let's say you have a bad habit of speaking negatively about yourself and you want to turn that into a good habit. You could say three positive affirmations about yourself every morning. In the evening, you could write down three things you did well that day. You could tell yourself 'well done' after you cook a nice meal. Or you could smile at yourself in the mirror when you get dressed.

Set mini-goals like this for yourself every day, and over time they become habit. I speak from experience here because practices like positive affirmations and gratitude didn't come naturally to me at first, but over time they became unshakable habits, like brushing my teeth. I wouldn't go to work without brushing my teeth, and I wouldn't go to work without listing things I'm grateful for. It's that ingrained in me. And these little habits help me achieve the bigger wins in life.

But listen, I know that building good habits takes work. So if you struggle to stay committed to your smaller goals, think back to your why (Chapter 5), because that is the foundation for everything you do. Your why should conjure up feelings of passion and excitement. You can use that passion to drive you forwards towards your goals. And conversely, you can use your mini-wins as a way to top up that passion, like topping up fuel on a long journey.

You can connect even the smallest of goals to your why. For example, let's say your why is something to do with a new career - a career that you've long dreamt of. Well, when you do achieve that amazing career, you're going to want to end each day of hard work by getting into a nicely made bed. So get in the habit of making your bed now! I'm using the bed example a lot, but there's a reason; studies have found that people who habitually make their bed are healthier, more confident, and more productive (among other positive attributes). The little things add up.

And if you really can't find a way to connect your mini-goals to your larger why, you could always come up with a new why just for that day. Your why could be as simple as getting through that particular day for your kids - in which case, getting through the day requires you to get up, make your bed, get dressed, and so on.

Like me, you could also use affirmations as a way to set mini-goals for yourself each day and build those positive habits. I find that just the simple process of verbalising an intention out loud makes me more likely to achieve it. In fact, this applies to big goals as much as little goals - why not create a list of affirmations that link to a range of your goals, big and small? For example:

- I am smart with money.
- I take care of my body and my body takes care of me.
- I am healthy.
- Every day I am building better habits.
- I use my time wisely.
- I am working towards the career of my dreams.
- Every day I get closer to my dream home.
- I will travel and have exciting experiences.
- I am curious and keen to learn.
- I am resilient. I am strong.
- I chase the things I want.
- I achieve my goals.

GOING AFTER THE BIGGER GOALS IN LIFE

Just as with small goals, your big goals must connect to your why. Goals stick when they stem from passion. Whereas if you strive for something that you *think* you should achieve – but you're not really passionate about it – you may struggle to stay committed to that journey. And why should you stay committed to something you're not passionate about?

So, with your why firmly in mind, try to create a picture of what you *really* want out of life. What specific goals will bring you joy and satisfaction?

The word 'specific' is key there. Goals must be specific and measurable. It's no good setting a goal of 'being rich' or 'being healthy'. What do those goals actually look like to you? A specific level of income per month, for example. The ability to run a half-marathon, perhaps. Be super-specific. Define what you really want to achieve.

Is it okay to set material goals or should you be focusing on some sort of lofty purpose? To my mind, it's fine to set material goals – such as a certain income goal – so long as you're clear on *why* you want to achieve that. As an example, I have a passive income goal (as in, how much monthly income I aim to earn from passive investments). But that goal is very much linked to my why. My why is freedom from the rat race, so I can enjoy quality time with my family and have more time for fun non-work stuff. I don't want that level of income just *because I can*; I want it because it connects to my why.

Another tip when it comes to setting big goals is to not worry too much - not right away - about *how* you'll achieve that goal. When you immediately get bogged down in the practicalities of how you'll achieve a goal, you may end up convincing yourself that you can't achieve it. You give up before you start. So don't impose those kinds of limits on yourself. Focus at first on clarifying exactly what you want, and why you want it. Then, once you feel fully committed to and passionate about a goal, you can begin to set out the specific actions and steps that will lead you to that goal. Which brings me to...

BIG GOALS ARE JUST A SERIES OF SMALL GOALS

Think of your goal as a roadmap. The end goal is the destination. So what landmarks are you looking for along the way? These are your mini-goals. Your practical action steps. The little wins that will lead you, bit by bit, to your destination.

Even the biggest, hairiest goal you can think of is really just a series of smaller goals. These smaller goals may be one-off goals (such as my friend Bill researching how to register a non-profit) or they may be habit-forming goals that you repeat every day (such as meditating to calm your mind and pave the way for success).

The important thing is to break your bigger goal (or goals) down into as many actionable steps as possible. Because, like a long road trip, you need those opportunities to fuel up along the way. Set your milestones too far apart and you risk getting lost on your journey or running out of fuel. Fill up on those little wins as often as you can.

This is just as applicable at any stage of life, not just on your journey back from rock bottom. My business partners and I have recently started a business called The Extraordinary Millionaire (www.extraordinarymillionaire.com), aiming to revolutionise the personal development and wealth education business. Seasoned entrepreneurs, we're used to going after big goals. But we still had to break this down into a series of smaller goals along the way. Attract the first 100 members, sell an initial piece of content, sell one seat on a training event, then sell 50 seats on a training event, and so on. One small, achievable goal leads to another. And the sum of many small achievable goals equals our big vision.

Whereas if we'd simply set a goal of attracting 10,000 members, with no smaller milestones leading up to that huge goal, there's a danger we could lose our enthusiasm or passion along the way.

None of this is groundbreaking stuff, of course. It's a time-honoured approach in business to break a goal down into smaller chunks. But this can be applied to any goal at all - lifestyle goals, financial goals, health goals, relationship goals, anything.

Let's say you have a specific financial goal in mind. You will want to break that down into mini-wins. One mini-win could be reading a book to learn a new investment technique. Another could be signing up for a course. Another could be finding and following the 10 best financial educators on YouTube. Another could be talking to a tax adviser.

You may need to plan your time carefully to accommodate these smaller goals. It's worth it, though. Use your time as wisely as you can. A train journey is an opportunity to learn something. Holidays are a great time to read. Walks can involve listening to a podcast. When I had a back operation and was facing a week in hospital (and more weeks laying up at home), I used that time to learn everything I could about crypto as a potential investment tool. Time that could have felt like a waste or 'dead space' ended up being incredibly valuable.

Basically, build those daily positive, productive habits that will help you progress along your journey. More on that coming up in Chapter 7.

COMMITTING YOUR GOALS TO PAPER

Putting your goals on paper helps to breathe life into them. It fosters that sense of commitment and clarity. And, if you're anything like me, just the simple act of getting something out of your head and onto paper brings a feeling of calmness.

As I've already mentioned, affirmations are a fantastic way to commit your goals to paper. Write your affirmations on post-it notes, in a notebook that you keep close at hand, or in an affirmations app – and each day, choose a few affirmations to say out loud. Remember to conjure the positive feelings that accompany your affirmation and *believe* in what you're saying (circle back to Chapter 3 for more on affirmations).

Remember Bill's bedside post-it note that said 'SAY THANK YOU' in big letters? You too can write prompts that help you complete mini-goals and build positive habits. If you want to make better food choices, for example, you could have a post-it note on the coffee jar that reminds you to eat a nourishing breakfast. You could have a reminder on your phone that prompts you to drink more water in the afternoon. You could pin lovely-looking recipes to your fridge to inspire you to cook something new each week.

Basically, create an environment around you that visually reminds you of your goals and supports your journey.

I also love using a dream board to commit my goals to paper and visually connect with my goals. Ideally your dream board will combine words with beautiful images that bring your goals to life. For instance, if one of your goals is to become fitter and healthier, you could include a picture of yourself when you were really happy in your physical self (or a picture of someone you think embodies physical wellness). Or if one of your goals is to start your own business, you could take a picture of your laptop set up in the garden, indicating the freedom to work whenever and wherever you like.

My own dream board includes pictures of destinations around the world where I'd love to take my family. My monthly passive income target is written on there. And there's a picture of a boat (that's a goal for when I'm older and want to spend less time on my businesses - which goes to show that goals can be short-term, medium-term, or even long-term. So long as they connect to your why).

But if you aren't much of a visual person, the images aren't essential. You could keep a simple written list of your goals somewhere where you'll see it often. In other words, the format of your dream board/goal list doesn't matter so much - what matters is that you refer to it often and use it as a tool to connect to your why, connect with your goals, and fuel your passion.

You could even use your dream board as part of your daily routine. In fact, I highly recommend that you do refer to your dream board daily. With regular use, the dream board focuses your mind on your goals. It can also serve as a useful prompt for visualising your goals. But we'll talk more about visualisation as a technique in Chapter 10.

BRING OTHERS ALONG ON YOUR JOURNEY

You know those people who can set a goal and relentlessly go after it, holding themselves accountable and needing no help from anyone else along the way? Annoying, aren't they? (I'm only joking. If you're one of those people, I salute you.)

The truth is, most of us need a little help in the accountability department. I know I do. I need others to help me stay focused on my goals.

At the simplest level, this just involves verbalising my goals with my family and friends. I talk openly about what I want to achieve and ask my loved ones to help keep me honest. Could you ask the same thing of your loved ones? If one of your goals is to retrain for a different career, for example, perhaps you could ask your partner to encourage you to spend an hour every evening studying – as opposed to beckoning you to the sofa with a wave of the remote control.

Another option is to buddy up with someone and commit to a goal together. Like having a gym partner or study buddy.

In other words, you need mechanisms to help keep you accountable. This is why people go to weight-loss groups and get weighed in a room full of strangers every week – because that weekly weigh-in, that accountability, keeps them on track throughout the rest of the week. Of course, many people find the sense of community at these groups helpful as well. But, let's be honest, it's the thought of the weekly weigh-in that shapes food choices across the week.

What's your equivalent of the weekly weigh-in? If you're aiming to write a novel, for example, you could join a writing group and commit to writing something every week to share with the group. Or you could commit to writing 5,000 words per week and have a chart on the kitchen fridge where you tick off that target each week (the adult equivalent of a chore sticker chart, perhaps). Your weekly win is there for everyone in the house to see.

If you really struggle to stay on track with your goals, another option is to hire a coach to keep you honest. Could be a fitness coach. Could be a business coach. I've worked with an accountability coach in the past – basically, a professional nag that chases me until I do the things I say I'm going to do! It's a fairly drastic option, and it's not for everyone, but I found it valuable.

Bottom line, don't underestimate the boost others can give to your goals. Whether it's friends and family or a professional coach, having the support of others can help you stay focused on what you want. They can also give you a kick up the backside when your actions don't support your goals.

LESSONS FOR THE CLIMB

- Yes, big life goals are important, but if you want to achieve the big things in life, you'd better get good at achieving the small things in life.
- Therefore, an important part of setting goals is learning to shift your mindset and find achievements in everyday places.
- This can be especially important when you're at rock bottom and even the thought of making your bed feels overwhelming. By achieving that mini-goal, you create a sense of pride and confidence, and you're more likely to complete the next mini-goal. And the cycle continues.
- Set mini-goals for yourself every day, and over time they become good habits that support your longer-term goals.
- Even big life goals are really just a series of mini-goals. In fact, it's vital you break huge goals down into chunks that are as manageable as possible. It makes the big goal feel more achievable, and you get to have lots of mini-wins as you work towards your end goal. Wins = confidence = continued enthusiasm.
- Make sure you connect your goals to your why. This is especially important for big goals. But even little goals can connect to a larger why. This will help you tap into a sense of passion, and keep the momentum going.
- Commit to your goals - big and small - both verbally and on paper. Affirmations and the dream board are really useful tools here.
- Where possible, encourage your loved ones to hold you accountable for your goals. Tell them what you're going to achieve and ask them to help keep you honest.

In Chapter 8 we'll talk about the importance of taking action towards your goals - especially that all-important first step. But before that, let's dwell a little more on the notion of good habits. How can you build a daily routine that supports your goals? Turn the page to find out.

Chapter 7

CREATING A ROUTINE THAT SUPPORTS YOUR JOURNEY

There's no straight line up from rock bottom. Rather, the journey twists and turns. Some days will be great. Others, not so much.

By this point in his journey, Bill was having more good days than bad days. Partly that was down to the healing power of time - a few months had passed since his wife left and he had grieved and adjusted to his new situation. But it was also because he had built a routine of positive habits and techniques that set him up to have more good days than bad. And when he did have a bad day, his routine gave him structure and strength. It didn't stop the fear or anxiety, but it helped him get through the day.

So in this chapter we're going to do something a little different. We're going to walk through a day in the life of our friend Bill, to understand the daily habits and techniques that helped him get to this point - the point where he had built a solid foundation for his future life.

A DAY IN THE LIFE OF BILL

Bill opened his eyes, smiled and said 'thank you' in his head. He was thankful just for waking up, for being alive. To extend that feeling, he spent a minute thinking of three things he was grateful for. On this day, he was grateful that he'd be picking up his daughter from her mum's later. He was grateful for the new recipe he'd tried last night, and decided he would cook it for Callie soon - she loved sweet potatoes. And as he stretched out his arms, Bill felt grateful for his physical body, the body that would literally carry him through this day.

When he'd first started his daily gratitude practice, at the request of his therapist, Bill wasn't convinced. But he now knew that listing just a few small things would stop his thoughts heading to a negative place first thing. And it was a handy reminder that even on his tough days, he still had things to be grateful for.

Then he got out of bed, opened the curtains, and let the natural light flood into his eyes. This was part of Bill's mission to improve his sleep. Bill had learned that getting natural light as early as possible in the morning tells the body to wake up and helps to regulate the circadian rhythm. So the simple act of throwing open his curtains first thing and absorbing the natural light was paving the way for more restful sleep later.

Bill made his bed with a little smile, joking to himself that he was already banking another little win for the day. He took care over this task, smoothing the bed neatly and plumping each pillow, because he knew that getting into a well-made bed in the evening would feel like a treat.

Downstairs, Bill drank a glass of water with a little lemon juice while he waited for the kettle to boil. After not drinking anything for eight hours, he was dehydrated. (We all are first thing.) So as much as he looked forward to his first coffee of the day, water came first. He'd found that drinking something hydrating first thing really helped to clear that morning brain fog – even more than his beloved caffeine.

Coffee in hand, Bill strolled to the armchair by the patio doors, so he could soak up even more natural light. He sipped his coffee, noticing the taste and smell each time he lifted the cup to his mouth. He cracked the doors open a little so he could hear the sounds of the neighbourhood (and the local birds) coming to life. These few mindful moments had become precious to Bill. He always used to drink his coffee on autopilot, taking hurried sips while making his breakfast and glancing at emails or social media. The radio would usually be on, bombarding him with bad news. But recently he'd started having his coffee in a more mindful way – no multitasking, no radio, just a few minutes of sitting, sipping and … noticing. He'd begun to look forward to his morning coffee more than ever. And not just for the shot of caffeine it delivered, but because it genuinely smelt and tasted better this way.

Bill had stopped listening to the news at all first thing in the morning. Same with social media. He would scan the news on his mid-morning break, and look at Facebook on his lunchbreak. But he no longer wanted to fill his brain with negative news from the second he woke up, because that would only lead to him noticing more negative things throughout the day.

Setting his empty coffee cup aside, Bill closed his eyes for a brief meditation. He didn't do this every day, but he tried to make time every other morning for a five-minute meditation. He sat in the armchair, eyes closed, clearing his mind. This hadn't come easy to Bill. When he'd first tried to meditate, his mind would fill with worries about the future. So he'd learned to focus on his breath in and out. 'One, two, three, four,' he would count in his head as he breathed in. 'One, two, three, four' as he exhaled. And on and on, for just a few minutes.

'Right,' Bill said, opening his eyes and standing. 'Today is going to be a great day. I am loved. I am working towards the life of my dreams.'

Bill said the words out loud, with the intention of carrying them through his day. When his daughter was around, Bill would say them privately in this head. But today, since he had the house to himself, he said the words aloud with confidence, welcoming the feelings of positivity and belief.

He thought for few seconds, then added, 'Today I'm going to brainstorm ideas for names for my charity. By the end of the day, I'm going to have five possible names.' And with that mini-goal set, it was time to start the day proper.

Bill liked to eat an hour or two after getting up rather than first thing. So he grabbed the tub of overnight oats that he'd prepared the night before, and packed the breakfast into his work bag, along with the other essentials for the day: lunch, protein bar, bottle of water, apple. On the way to the gym, he listened to a podcast about foraging (he'd subscribed to several podcasts that were relevant to his charity idea). And at the gym, he plugged in his headphones and pressed play on his 'happy tunes' playlist. He'd had fun creating a playlist of his favourite songs, and each time he played it, it lifted his mood.

Bill aimed to go to the leisure centre three mornings a week – alternating between rowing, weights and swimming, depending on how his body felt that day. But more importantly, he had been building all sorts of movement into his daily routine. He'd stretch in bed first thing. He'd park a little further from the office. He'd go for a stroll on his lunchbreak. He took the office stairs and would break into a little run up the stairs when no one was looking. And while sat at his desk, he'd take note of how long he'd been sitting still. If it had been an hour since he last stood, he'd stop what he was doing – no matter how important it was – and take a walk to the office kitchen, or simply stand and stretch a little. He'd try to do this across the day. Tonight, he planned to cut the grass in the garden and do half an hour's weeding. His wife had been the gardener in their marriage and Bill was surprised at how gardening worked his muscles and left him feeling tired (in a good way). He felt momentarily grateful for all the new things he was learning about gardening.

Bill's morning at his corporate job was much the same as usual. He answered emails, led a team meeting, caught up with a couple of his direct reports, and looked at the CVs HR had sent over for a job vacancy in his team. It was a typical Thursday morning. Nothing exciting. In quiet moments, Bill's mind wandered and he visualised swapping the office for the woods. 'I am working towards the life of my dreams,' he said, and wrote a reminder to brainstorm potential names for his charity.

Lunch on this day was leftovers from the night before: sweet potato curry. (The beauty of cooking on the days he didn't have his daughter – there were always plenty of leftovers.) He'd found it difficult to eat healthily when he was really down, back in the early days of the split, often relying on processed foods and takeaways. But he found that over-reliance on processed foods affected more than just his waistline – his energy levels would swing wildly and he'd feel irritable. Bill had reached a point where he wanted to be more in control of his energy and moods, so he tried to prepare food from scratch as much as possible. He'd take a homemade lunch into work most days (even if it was just a sandwich). But on days when that didn't work out, he didn't beat himself up about it – he'd enjoy browsing the range of lunch options on offer at the local Marks & Spencer, taking care over his choice.

Over lunch, he spent a fun 30 minutes scrawling potential business names down on his phone: The Wild Foundation, Acorns to Oaks, Groundworks, Find Your Footing, Restore Through Nature...

In the afternoon, Bill had to work on his budget forecast for the next year. His superiors in the American head office (Bill's employer was a multinational consultancy firm) were expecting his finalised budget by the end of tomorrow, and he still had plenty to do. So when one of his team members knocked on his office door and said there was a problem, Bill groaned. One of their top clients was requesting an urgent meeting, but their client manager was off sick. Bill would have to stand in and lead the meeting in their place - leaving no time for finishing his budget.

Bill took a breath. Two months ago, he would have muttered something like, 'Why is this happening to me? I don't need this today.' But Bill was learning to flip negative thoughts into more positive ones. 'Why is this happening *for* me?' he thought to himself. The answer, he decided, was the universe teaching him that he'd need to be extra flexible and able to think on his feet if he was going to run a successful non-profit. This was good practice. It was still a little annoying, especially as he'd have to come in early tomorrow to finish his budget. But he wasn't going to let it ruin his afternoon - something that would have easily happened two months ago. This subtle mindset shift moved him from a victim of his circumstances to someone in control of his thoughts and actions. It was a powerful shift and one that made him feel thankful.

That evening, Bill and Callie went out for ramen - her favourite. It had been a long day and the meal kit dinner that Bill had been planning to cook could wait until tomorrow. After doing a little work in the garden, Bill watched a movie with Callie - really paying attention to the film instead of simultaneously scrolling on his phone. They pulled the curtains and turned the lights in the living room down low, partly to create that cinema feel, but also to ease their bodies into nighttime mode (there's that circadian rhythm again). And once Callie had gone to bed, Bill spent a peaceful half an hour clearing up the downstairs while finishing his foraging podcast. There would be no more screen time for him until the next day. Lastly, Bill prepared breakfast for the next morning - overnight oats times two, with frozen blueberries for his daughter and frozen strawberries for him.

In bed, Bill listed a few good things that had happened that day, including handling the unscheduled client meeting with ease. To Bill, this felt like wiping the slate clean and getting his brain ready for the next day. And finally, Bill picked up the book next to his bed - an inspiring story of someone hiking the Appalachian Trail in America - and read for 20 minutes by the cosy light of his bedside lamp. He felt tired, in a good way, and ready for a restful night's sleep.

WHAT DOES A DAY IN YOUR LIFE LOOK LIKE?

As you can see, Bill's daily routine pulls together the techniques and practices we've talked about so far in this book: gratitude, positive affirmations, mindfulness and meditation, setting big and small goals, taking care of your physical self (through sleep, nutrition and exercise), and generally making time for yourself. (In Chapter 10 we'll cover more forward-looking mindset tools that will help you on your journey.)

How can you create a daily routine that supports your journey from rock bottom? It doesn't have to look like Bill's. Maybe you hate the gym and would rather just walk the dog after work. That's great. Maybe meditation isn't your jam at all. No problem, how about ten minutes of reading or deadheading roses in the garden? Anything mindful that pulls you into the moment at hand and creates time for yourself is beneficial.

It's a bit like gathering your tools for a job. Except the job is having the best day you can, and the tools are, basically, good habits. You want to build the habits that will help you ace the good days and manage the bad days with more confidence.

But to be clear, Bill had built his routine over a period of time, little by little. We're not talking about ripping up your current daily routine and changing everything all at once - in fact, you probably shouldn't do that. Instead, make little changes that are easy to stick to, like making your bed in the morning, drinking your morning tea or coffee more mindfully, and eating a nutritious breakfast. After a while, these little tricks will become second nature, and you can build the next little change into your routine, and so on and so on. Over time, you build a structure or framework of supportive habits.

I can't tell you what you should and shouldn't do in your daily routine to bring you happiness and success. What you need may be very different to Bill. My own routine starts with gratitude, as it does with Bill - but I have other morning practices that I love to do most days, including looking at my dream board and doing some visualisation (we'll talk more about visualisation in Chapter 10). You may not want to do any of these things in the morning - maybe you hate mornings and are more of a night owl. You do you.

If you don't get to do all of your good habits on a given day, don't beat yourself up about it. I typically meditate a few times a week, but lately that's not been the case. My family and I have moved house three times in as many months while we wait for a house purchase to go through. Honestly, my morning routine has been all over the place. But we'll talk more about that later.

The important thing is, I know that tools like meditation are there for me when I need them, because I took the time to *build those habits* in the first place. Meditation is like riding a bike for me now - I don't have to relearn how to do it, just because I haven't done it in a while. Therefore, I strongly recommend you take time to build the habits that work for you, so they're always there in your toolkit whenever you need them - even if you don't do them every day for the rest of your life.

The only set-in-stone rule that I want to stress is to dedicate time to what you need. Carve out that time for yourself. Commit to good practices like eating well, moving your body, building good sleep habits, being mindful and thankful, and so on. Commit to developing yourself so that you can successfully make that climb from rock bottom. Commit to the process. Even when life is busy. Especially when life is busy.

MY TIPS FOR STICKING TO YOUR ROUTINE

The first step is to build your own unique routine that works for you, whatever (and whenever) that looks like. But when it comes to sticking to your routine, the following might help:

- Stay focused on your 'why'. Why do you want to build a better life for yourself? Keep reminding yourself of your why and use that as fuel for your journey. Connect even small habits and goals to your why.
- Create a dream board and pin it up somewhere prominent, where you'll see it every day. I know I've mentioned the dream board a couple of times, but it's such a useful tool. I find it delivers a shot of inspiration and excitement every time I look at it. Plus, it helps to focus my attention and energy on the things I want most in life.
- Be kind to yourself. If you let your routine slip a bit, or it's taking longer than you expected to build a positive habit – don't react from a place of negativity or frustration. Being hard on yourself isn't constructive, and you're only attracting more negativity your way. Just be kind. Remind yourself of how far you've come and recommit to the journey ahead.
- Stop being 'busy'. Because being busy isn't the same as doing important things. How many times do you find yourself prioritising being busy over doing the things that really *matter* to you? ('I don't have time for X because I'm busy doing Y and Z.') Prioritise the things that are important in the context of your longer-term journey (which could be simple things like eating better and moving more). Prioritise those. The busy work will still be there later.

WHEN THE ROUTINE REALLY DOES GO OUT THE WINDOW

Okay, sometimes life happens and your fabulous, carefully-crafted routine gets obliterated. I mentioned that my family and I have moved three times in three months while we wait for our new home to be ready. Let me tell you, finding time for my normal routine has been *hard*.

To overcome this, I remind myself that my routine is simply about finding time and space for myself. And I can do that in many ways, even if it's not in my usual ways. For example, I can do a quick breathing exercise before a meeting. It's not my typical meditation, but it's still helpful. Or if I was too tired to write any of my book yesterday, I can make some voice notes during my lunch break today. I can carve out these micro-chunks of time that allow me to move forwards towards my goals. And sometimes I just have to say to my kids, 'Guys, Daddy needs ten minutes of quiet time' so I can calm my noisy brain. I'll set a timer if I have to.

It may also help to literally diarise things that matter to you. If I know I've got a really hectic work day coming up, I might block out 20 minutes in the middle of that day to go for a walk. If I didn't put it in my calendar, I might not do it. I'll also set regular reminders that tell me to stretch or say thank you. Sounds funny, but it really helps.

Most of all, remember that one 'bad' day - a day where you neglect your habits and routine - doesn't have to lead to a 'bad' week. Tomorrow is a new day. A new chance to start again and recommit to the things you want.

You'll find more tips for staying motivated in Chapter 11.

THE IMPORTANCE OF BECOMING A LIFELONG LEARNER

At the very start of this book, I introduced my concept of the Extraordinary Millionaire - someone who focuses on abundance, rather than just money.

Someone who is thankful for all the things they have in the present while they strive for a better future. Someone who understands the power of mindset and shapes their thoughts accordingly. And yes, someone who builds a routine of success-boosting habits. In this way, you can live like an Extraordinary Millionaire even when you're not a millionaire - when you're not even close to being a millionaire. I certainly did. Because it's not about having pots of money and driving a fancy car. It's about being Extraordinary.

And one of the best ways you can be Extraordinary is to get really bloody curious. Get super-passionate about learning new things. Become a lifelong learner. Because an Extraordinary Millionaire is something who's continually learning, rather than thinking they know everything.

Your goals may take you on a formal learning journey - such as studying for a new qualification, taking courses that help you turn a hobby into a business, or even taking swimming lessons! Formal education and structured lessons are great, but I also encourage you to seek learning opportunities wherever you can. Listen to informative podcasts. Watch TED talks. Seek out and follow experts on social media. Join forums. Go to talks and educational events. Sign up for newsletters on relevant topics. Read books that educate and inspire you. (By the way, if you're keen to boost your financial education, we have a helpful reading list on the Extraordinary Millionaire site www.extraordinarymillionaire.com.)

Basically, immerse yourself in new topics, whether it's starting a business, investing in property, learning yoga, vegetarian cooking, whatever. Immerse yourself and enjoy the process of using your brain in new ways. It's another way to get those confidence-boosting mini-wins on your journey from rock bottom.

I honestly believe that learning is the secret ingredient for success - whatever success looks like to you. If you're going to build the life of your dreams, you have to become an information sponge. When I went from renting out a spare room in my first home, to me moving out and turning the whole house into an HMO (house in multiple occupation - where the bedrooms are rented individually to tenants, instead of renting the whole house on one contract), I had to learn about the myriad of rules and regulations about HMOs. Then, once I'd got a few successful HMOs under my belt, I started developing properties with the intention of converting them into HMOs. Which meant I had to learn the ins and outs of property development and project management. Then I began to tackle bigger developments - like converting office blocks into apartments - which meant I had to learn new ways of finding funding and partnering with wealthy investors. And all the while I've been learning mindset techniques like visualisation, and business skills like leadership.

What's more, your learning journey doesn't end when you achieve success. Far from it. I'm still learning all the time - how to be a better writer, how to build my personal brand, how to present information on camera...

I consider myself a lifelong learner. Emphasis on the *lifelong*. 'Never stop learning' has become a motto for me. As you work to build your own routine of positive habits, I urge you to make learning a key part of it.

LESSONS FOR THE CLIMB

- Aim to create a routine of regular habits and practices that support your journey from rock bottom - a routine which may include some or all of the techniques we've talked about so far in this book: good nutrition, good sleep habits, exercise and movement, positive affirmations, gratitude, mindfulness and meditation, and setting big and small goals for yourself.
- You want to build the habits that will help you ace the good days and manage the bad days with more confidence.
- Your routine should be unique to you. If you're a night owl, build your routine around that. If you're a chipper morning person, build new habits into the morning routine.
- Remember that your success-boosting routine is really just about making time for yourself and taking care of yourself as you work

towards your goals. So even if your routine falls apart on occasion, you can still find micro-ways to make time for yourself.
- I also urge you to make continual learning a part of your routine, whether it's a formal education route, or informal learning through books, podcasts, forums, etc. Learning is the secret ingredient for success - whatever success looks like to you - so cultivate that thirst for knowledge.

While we're on the subject of learning, don't fall into the trap of thinking that, just because you can't do something (yet), or don't know how to do something (yet), that you'll never be able to do it. I know that fear of failure can hold a lot of people back from trying new things but I promise you, anything can be learned and improved with time and effort. Anything at all. In the next chapter, we'll explore this concept of fear - or why you should feel the fear, and, as the saying goes, do it anyway!

Chapter 8

OVERCOMING FEAR AND TAKING THE FIRST STEP

Bill was doing great in so many ways. He was adjusting to his new life as a solo parent. His daughter was thriving. They'd even gone on a little family holiday together. I knew it was something that Bill had been nervous about (he was worried that going on a family holiday would only remind him that his family had changed). But they'd had an amazing time in Cornwall, learning to surf and exploring the coastline. Bill had come back looking refreshed, tanned and relaxed.

I was happy to see him and his daughter settling into life together. But I wondered why he didn't seem ready to start working towards his career-change goal. Bill had uncovered his why - his desire to turn his rock bottom experience into something positive and help other people in need. He seemed so passionate about it at the time. And yet, he hadn't taken any notable steps towards it.

THE FIRST STEP CAN BE A SCARY ONE

By this point, Bill had been skirting around the charity idea for more than a month - doing a little reading here, brainstorming a few ideas there. But he hadn't committed to it fully. He hadn't registered the business or started fundraising or started connecting with people who could help him run wilderness trips. He'd told me he wanted to meet with the local council to potentially get their support, but hadn't made a call or reached out to anyone.

I was confused. This was Bill's purpose. His mission. This was going to form a major part of his future life. Why wasn't he grabbing it with both hands and taking that first step?

When I was at rock bottom, I couldn't wait to put as much distance as possible between myself and rock bottom. True, I was much younger then. I didn't have a family at that point, and I'd only just met the woman who would become my wife. I had fewer responsibilities, less to lose. In fact, I'd already lost most of the things I could lose. Which is how I found myself in that crappy flat in Dover with the desire to get as far away as possible, as quickly as possible.

Bill's situation was different. He was in his late forties, with a child, a comfortable financial setup, and a lot to lose. But I didn't want to see Bill give up on his dream of being his own boss again, helping others, and finding a sense of community. I wanted that for him. And so I plucked up the courage to have one of those 'tough love' conversations with Bill. I was going to tell him that he needed to get his arse in gear.

Yet, when I arrived at his house, bearing Sunday morning coffee and croissants, Bill beat me to it. Like he knew what I was coming to say.

'I know what you're going to say,' Bill said, opening the bag of croissants and taking a sniff.

'What?' I asked, innocently.

'You're going to ask me about the charity and why I haven't done anything about it yet.'

'Well...' I said, my pause giving me away.

'You're right,' Bill said. 'I've been dragging my feet. I kept making excuses in the runup to the holiday. There's no point doing much before we go away, etc. etc. I promised myself I'd make a proper start when we came back.'

'And you've been back two weeks....'

'Exactly. But it all came to a head last night.'

'How so?' I asked.

'I don't know if it's because I knew you were coming over today, or the timing just felt right, but I picked up that book yesterday.' He nodded at a book sitting on the kitchen table. 'I started reading it yesterday lunchtime and devoured the whole thing in a day.'

The book was *Feel the Fear and Do It Anyway*, by Susan Jeffers.

RECOGNISING THE FEAR

'I love this book,' I said, picking it up and flipping the pages like a deck of cards.

'I've had it in my office for years but never got around to reading it,' Bill admitted. 'But yesterday, it just called to me. It's like a voice inside was saying, "It's time, Bill. Finally, it's time."'

'Time to read it?'

'Time to start living the life I want,' Bill clarified.

He continued. 'I was sat in that armchair last night, having read the last page and it was like everything made sense. This book shone a light on the one last thing holding me back from moving forward. Something so powerful and ingrained in me it's probably influenced most of the decisions I've made in my life. Something that's hardwired into all of us, but something we're quick to hide.'

'Go on,' I encouraged him.

'Fear' Bill said, simply. 'It hit me last night. I'm scared. Scared to take that first step into the unknown. I mean, life these past few months hasn't exactly been a barrel of laughs, but at least I know what I'm dealing with. I've been strangely comfortable in this little world of pain and grief. In a way, it's easier than dealing with an unknown future. I have this vision in my head of what I want to achieve, but I have no idea if it'll pan out that way. What if I end up bankrupt and miserable? Where will we live? How will I put Callie through university?'

I nodded. 'I get it. It's natural to feel afraid of the unknown. Or feel afraid when you lack confidence. But it shouldn't stop you moving towards your goals.'

'Easy for you to say,' Bill said. 'You're self-confidence personified.'

'I feel fear all the time!' I said.

FEAR IS UNIVERSAL

'I feel fear every time I embark on a new business venture,' I said. 'I feel fear about being a good parent. I feel fear about losing my comfortable lifestyle. I feel fear about getting older, getting sick, you name it. Fear for me takes all kinds of shapes, from vague worries about the future to specific phobias that affected me for years.'

'Phobias?' Bill asked.

'Did I ever tell you I was terrified of public speaking?'

'But you do it all the time!'

I nodded. 'Now I do. And I'm much more comfortable with it these days. But I didn't used to be. I've been afraid of speaking in front of others my whole life, all through school, university... I remember my second year at uni I had to give a presentation on some engineering topic and it was the most scared I'd ever felt. I was shaking, nearly sick. It was all I thought about for days. And on the day itself, I was so scared of forgetting what I had to say, I literally did the whole presentation with my face buried in my notes, reading the words off the page one by one. I was the worst presentation of the day by a mile. I wouldn't be surprised if I was the worst speaker my lecturers had ever seen.'

'I can't imagine you being like that,' Bill laughed.

'But at the same time,' I went on, 'I could see how public speaking could be kind of fun. I saw some of my classmates being so relaxed about it and seemingly enjoying the process of presenting. I was so jealous. I wanted to be that way. The next time I had to speak in public wasn't until my brother's wedding. And I was desperate to enjoy it. I didn't want to spend the whole wedding feeling sick and terrified.'

'So what did you do?' Bill asked.

'I read this tip that said the key to being a relaxed speaker is just to know your subject matter inside out. And it made so much sense. Part of why I was so nervous in that uni presentation was because I didn't know the topic well enough. But when it came to talking about my brother and his embarrassing escapades? I didn't need to worry about forgetting what I wanted to say because I knew all the stories inside out. It helped me relax into it. I was still a bit nervous, obviously, but I felt a lot more confident. And ultimately, I really enjoyed standing there taking the piss out of my brother. I did a whole PowerPoint slideshow and everything.'

'And that helped you get over your fear?'

I nodded. 'I realised that, for me, feeling prepared and knowing my subject matter is key to overcoming my fears. And now, I can talk for England about my area of expertise. I present property courses in front of complete strangers. I've presented for TV and YouTube. And I can relax about it, because I know the knowledge is in my head. I feel well-prepared.'

'I'm not sure how to translate that to my situation, though,' Bill said. 'I'm scared of quitting my job, starting a charity that fails, and ending up destitute.'

THE FIRST STEP IS JUST THE FIRST STEP...

'But you're trying to think about the whole picture at once,' I said, 'which is a lot to prepare for. No wonder you feel overwhelmed. All you really need to do is take the first step. The first step isn't quitting your job and immediately heading off into the woods. Your first step is, say, setting up a website so you can start contacting potential donors and partners. That's all it is at first. Look, I'm not saying the big picture isn't important. Of course you need a roadmap of where you're heading. But that roadmap doesn't mean anything if you don't take the first step. You can't set goals and wait for the universe to drop them in your lap. You have to actively move towards what you want.'

I continued. 'If you're anything like me, you'll get a confidence boost from feeling as prepared as possible. Like me knowing my subject matter for a speech. For you, that might be learning as much as you can about running a charity and refreshing your wilderness skills. Like, when I decided to quit my job and become a full-time property investor, my first step wasn't buying a property to develop. My first step was going to property seminars so I could learn about different property strategies. My first step was immersing myself in the topic as much as I could.'

'I see...' Bill said.

'The first step is rarely *doing* the actual thing that scares you. It's doing something that paves the way. Your first step isn't quitting your job. That's a long way down the road. So what exactly is your first step?' I asked.

Bill thought for a few seconds. 'Probably finalising my charity name, and hiring a web designer to sort the website. Set up an email address, that sort of thing.'

'Doesn't sound too scary to me. I'll give you my web designer's details if you like.'

'You're right,' Bill nodded. 'It's not that bad when I think about it.'

'And even if that first step does feel daunting, you could make it less daunting by looking at websites you admire and making a list of features you like. Things you want to emulate in your own website. That's a good way to feel prepared for talking to a web designer.'

'I like it,' Bill nodded.

I took a last bite of my croissant. 'This fear you're feeling, Bill, it's natural. But make it the last thing you feel at rock bottom. From here, you're starting your climb.'

'Feel the fear and do it anyway,' Bill said.

'Well, how about feel the fear, prepare as best you can, *then* do it anyway?'

'Better,' Bill nodded.

TAKING YOUR FIRST STEP

Even the longest journey starts with a single step. The same is true of your journey, whatever it may be.

That first step is scary. It will probably take you outside of your comfort zone. It may feel like a leap of faith or a leap into the unknown. But remember, it's just one step.

Say you want to escape a pattern of toxic relationships and find a loving partner. The first step isn't walking up to a beautiful stranger and asking them out. The first step might be working on loving and taking care of yourself - which might mean joining a local walking group or signing up for art classes. In time, once you've expanded your social circle, built hobbies you love, and built your confidence, you might then sign up for a dating app or ask someone out for a coffee. But the first step is just the first step.

On that Sunday, Bill reached out to a web designer to get his website started. It was a small step, but significant. Because he was now truly ready to begin his climb from rock bottom.

What's that first step you can take towards your future? Signing up for a course, perhaps. Going to a networking meeting. Enquiring about therapy. Dusting off your CV. Buying a pair of running shoes. Downloading a nutrition app. Researching something... When you really think about it, your first step might not be that daunting at all.

WHY THAT FIRST (SMALL) STEP IS SO IMPORTANT

You can't just write your goals down, create a dream board, say your affirmations and ... wait for the universe to deliver your desire, like it's a chicken vindaloo. You have to take action. This book will help you on your journey but only if you take that first step.

Action is the difference between a dream and a goal. Without action, it'll only ever be a dream. But once you start taking action, no matter how small that first step is, your dream becomes a goal - something you're actively working towards. How cool is that?

In Chapter 6 I said that even the biggest goal is really just a series of smaller goals. Now's a good time to remember that. Your first step is just a mini-goal that leads in the right direction.

Easily said, right? But if you're anything like my friend Bill, there might be something holding you back from taking that first step: fear.

FEAR IS NATURAL

Fear is inbuilt in all of us to keep us safe. Humans evolved to feel fear so we could predict and protect against the possibility of danger. Imagine you're hiking in a forest and you see a dark cave ahead. Rationally you know there probably isn't a bear or big cat in that cave. At least, not here in the UK. And yet that fear is still deep inside you. Because millions of years ago there might well have been a dangerous predator lurking in an environment like that.

That is the big problem with our inbuilt, primal fear - it's designed for a world that most of us no longer live in. Obviously, that primal fear can be useful. Walking down an unknown dark street at night, fear will heighten your senses and keep you alert. But as Susan Jeffers explains in *Feel the Fear and Do It Anyway*, that inbuilt fear doesn't know the difference between a potentially life-threatening situation and an opportunity to grow. The brain just sees something different and unknown, and it automatically shows you every possible thing that could go wrong.

Your brain wants to convince you that changing the status quo is dangerous. As such, it will fill your mind with every possible reason why you *shouldn't* do something. It does this to keep you safe. But when it comes to escaping rock bottom, you're going to have to put yourself in unknown territory. You're going to have to take chances and grab this opportunity to grow. You're going to have to learn to feel the fear and do it anyway.

FEAR CAN BE A POSITIVE MOTIVATOR

I like to distil my motivations down into two categories. There's the 'If I don't do X then Y will happen. And Y is bad.' This is a feeling that pushes me to do something because I know if I don't do it, there will be negative consequences. Like when I used to leave my homework until the very last minute as a child. At that point, I was motivated to do it because I knew there'd be hell to pay if my parents got a call from my teacher. I think of this as a 'push' motivator. If I know that not replying to my accountant by a certain deadline might result in me getting a fine from HMRC, then you'd better believe I'm going to reply by that deadline. It's the push I need to do it. And it's often based on a kind of fear - albeit a helpful fear.

The other motivator is more of a pull effect. It's the feeling of 'I want to do this for me, because I want to succeed'. This is what motivates me to write books like this, expand my mentorship programmes and work on becoming a better presenter. I'm pulled towards goals like this, not because I'm afraid of the consequences of *not* doing them, but because I'm excited about the possibilities of actually doing them.

Personally, I find both types of motivator work for me. Both are useful. Both have their place. But you may naturally lean more one way than the other. If you do lean a certain way, how can you use that to your advantage? Can you harness your preferred style of motivator to achieve the things you want?

If you need a push motivator to get you off your butt, how can you work with that, rather than fight against it? Let's say Bill required a push to send him on his way - in that case, he could tell his web designer that he'd have a full website brief delivered to her by the end of the week. If Bill didn't deliver all the info she needed on time, he'd lose his slot and his website would be delayed.

If you're more motivated by pull factors, you can also use that to your advantage. One way might be to flip a fear on its head and turn it into a positive scenario that motivates you. Bill, for instance, was afraid of his charity being a failure. Flipping that scenario on its head, Bill could visualise his charity as a wild success - helping hundreds or thousands of men through their darkest period in life and ultimately becoming one of the best-known mental health charities in the UK.

Basically, understand what motivates you. Understand whether you're the kind of person who might actually be motivated by fear - at least in certain scenarios - or whether you're better served by flipping fear on its head. Learn when to use each response to your advantage.

TIPS FOR OVERCOMING YOUR FEAR

Fear of failure is perhaps the biggest thing that holds many people back. But it might help to remember that the most successful people in the world don't avoid failure - they just know how to get back up when things don't go their way. They have the blueprint for escaping rock bottom. If they lose everything, they know they can get it all back again.

Think of this book as your blueprint for escaping rock bottom. Yes, things might not always go to plan on your journey towards a better life. But the tools in this book can be applied time and time again, through small setbacks and big life challenges.

Successful people also know that failure is just another opportunity to learn and grow. Each failure, big or small, is just another milestone on the road to achieving the life they desire. So rather than avoiding failure (by avoiding taking that first step) try to embrace the possibility that you will probably fail at some things, and that's okay. It's all part of learning and improving.

This is what psychologist and bestselling author Carol Dweck calls the 'growth mindset'. Someone with a growth mindset sees failures and setbacks as part of growth. Whereas someone with a 'fixed mindset' will avoid challenges to avoid failing in the first place. Which is why so many people end up never taking the first step towards their goals.

Even if you naturally lean more towards a fixed mindset, don't worry. The good news is you can learn to adopt a growth mindset. Reading Dweck's book *Mindset* is a great start. But here are some other tips for learning to overcome fear of failure or fear of the unknown:

- **Remind yourself of things you've done right in your life.** When you're at a low point in life, it can be hard to remember that it's not always been this way - you've done plenty of things right in your life. Rock bottom does not define you.
- **Practise stepping outside of your comfort zone.** Find small ways to push yourself beyond your comfort zone and take mini-risks. You could, for example, try a new physical activity, like indoor snowboarding, or practise speaking your mind more often (instead of biting your tongue for an easy life).
- **Build your creative muscles.** Creative thinking can help you solve problems, be more adaptable, and respond well when things don't go to plan. So find little ways to boost your creativity in everyday life. Even if it's as simple as doing a puzzle, doodling, or colouring in a colouring book.
- **Learn, learn, learn.** Often we're scared of something or lack confidence because we just don't feel prepared. So what can you do to prepare yourself mentally (or physically) for your initial steps? The mindset techniques in this book are great for boosting your confidence and preparedness. But you may also need to make time for formal learning, practising a specific skill, or whatever links to your goal.
- **Go easy on yourself.** When things do go wrong, it's obviously helpful to examine what happened so you can learn from the experience and do better in future. But that's not the same thing as berating yourself. Don't be hard on yourself if you fail. Failing at something doesn't mean *you're a failure* or you're inherently flawed. It's just part of the process.

And finally, there's one more huge thing you can do to overcome your fear of the unknown...

ASK YOURSELF, WHAT'S THE WORST THAT WILL HAPPEN?

If you're avoiding taking action towards your goals, this exercise can be super-helpful. It's all about overcoming your brain's primal fear by fighting it with good old-fashioned logic.

Ask yourself, 'What's the worst that could happen?'

That's it. What's the worst that could happen if you move to a new country, accept that job offer, start a new business, start dating, start writing a novel, or sign up for a marathon? What is the thing you fear the most? Pinpoint the specific scenario that holds you back from taking the first step.

Then – and this is the crucial bit – ask yourself, 'Okay, if that's the worst that can happen, how will I deal with it if it does happen. How will I move forward in a positive way?'

It might help here to think about whether you've been through a similar scenario before and how you moved through it then. And if you haven't ever found yourself in the specific situation you fear, I bet that someone else has. Someone you know, someone you read about, someone you heard about. Did they survive? (I'm assuming the answer is yes.) What steps did they take?

You've now identified the worst that could happen and reassured yourself that, even if it does happen, you will (in all probability) survive it. (If your goal genuinely involves a threat to your survival, maybe think twice!) You've also got a rough plan B.

Now you can weigh up that worst-case scenario against the option of doing nothing at all. What's the worst that will happen if you *don't* take steps towards your goal? What will happen if you don't attempt to climb up from rock bottom?

The answer is you'll still be where you are now, rock bottom. In a month's time, a year's time, in 10 years' time. Nothing will change. Is that really better than your worst-case scenario? I bet, on reflection, the real worst case is you *not* taking action.

Remember, fear is a natural part of change and growth. It's okay to feel afraid of taking that first step. It's your brain's defence system. Be thankful for it. But know that it's up to you to differentiate between the things that are scary because they genuinely threaten your safety, and the things that are scary because they're simply unknown. And the unknown could be the greatest opportunity of your life.

LESSONS FOR THE CLIMB

- It's vital you take action towards your goals. You can't just set a goal and wait for it to happen for you.
- Taking the first step towards your new life can feel scary. Usually because of a fear of failure or simply a fear of the unknown. This is natural.
- It may help to remember that the first step is just that - the *first* step. The first step isn't usually a case of jumping in and doing the thing that scares you. The first step is typically a small thing that moves you closer to your goal. The first step could be as simple as making a phone call or sending an email.
- Fear can sometimes be a positive motivator that pushes you to do something you've been putting off. But if that kind of motivator doesn't work for you, try flipping your fear on its head. Instead of picturing things going wrong, picture the very best outcome you can imagine.
- There are little steps you can take to overcome fear. For example, you can practise stepping outside of your comfort zone. You can flex your creative muscles. And you can work on your preparedness through continual learning.
- And when all else fails, ask yourself, what's the worst that could happen if you do take that first step? What is the worst that could

happen - and how will you deal with it? Then weigh up that scenario against the option of doing nothing at all. Chances are, the thought of doing nothing is scarier than the prospect of taking action.

It's true that each journey begins with a single step, but we all know that there will be many more steps after that. The challenge lies in staying focused on one step at a time and not getting overwhelmed by the big picture. How can you do that? Turn to the next chapter to find out.

Part III: The Climb Itself

NAVIGATING THE JOURNEY FROM ROCK BOTTOM

'**To get through the hardest journey and continue living,** we need to take only one step at a time; but we must keep on stepping.'

—CHINESE PROVERB

Chapter 9

STAYING FOCUSED ON ONE STEP AT A TIME

Bill was on his journey, moving towards his goal of running a successful non-profit. He had registered his charity. He had set up a website and email address. He had taken wilderness survival and first aid courses. He had been learning more about meditation as a potential tool to use on his trips with clients. He'd planned out structured events and trips, scouted locations, and more. He was making progress.

But Bill was struggling with fundraising. He'd had some positive first meetings with potential donors, and he'd even managed to get a foot in the door with his local council. Yet things were not moving as fast as he would like. Turns out, when it comes to getting people and organisations to part with their money, things move slowly! Bill was frustrated and - since he was juggling all this alongside his corporate job - he was tired.

'Maybe I should just put it all on hold for now,' he said to me. 'It's harder than I imagined.'

'Are you still seeing your therapist?' I asked him.

'Couple times a month. Why?'

'What does she say about coping with frustrations and bumps in the road?'

Bill replied, 'She says that even climbing Mount Everest is a question of putting one foot in front of the other. Over and over again, one step at a time. It's not always helpful to think about reaching the summit; sometimes you just have to focus on the next step, then the step after that.'

'Like Rocky,' I said. 'You know, "One day at a time, one punch at a time, one round at a time." It's good advice.'

Bill smiled, 'I guess so. But I so desperately want to reach the summit. I want this charity up and running so I can help others. And, of course, so I can quit my job and be my own boss again ... Are you listening to me?'

The word 'running' had triggered a memory in me and I was looking around Bill's living room for a specific photograph. I walked over to his bookshelf, picked up the framed photo and took it over to him.

The photo was of Bill crossing the finish line of the Jurassic Coast 100km ultramarathon. In the photo he looked battered, as weary as anyone could look, but elated.

'Remember this day?' I asked.

Bill took the photo in his hand. 'God, how could I forget. One of the best and worst experiences of my life.'

'Tell me about that day,' I said.

WHAT IT'S REALLY LIKE TO RUN AN ULTRAMARATHON

This is what Bill told me:

'I started that day feeling so strong and confident. I knew I'd prepared well. I'd spent a lot of time on my training, done the miles. I'd also planned the route well, set my time goals, and targeted on the map where I wanted to be and when. I was ready. So when I stood there on the start line with 100km of the unknown ahead of me, I felt exhilarated and excited. I was full of thoughts of the finish line and how it would feel to have completed 100km. In my mind I had the perfect event laid out in front of me. Everything would go just as I planned. I was ready, I was prepared.

I was wrong.

The gun went off, the race started and those first few minutes were pure chaos. There's nothing quite like the start of a marathon. It's so crowded as hundreds of competitors all start off at the same time. You bump into others and get jostled yourself. You struggle to find your own space in the crowd and, because of that, your pace is totally inconsistent.

I'd look at my watch one minute and think "I'm going too fast; I need to slow my pace." Then the next minute I'd be going too slow. All my good planning seemed to go straight out the window. I started to feel the tiniest flicker of panic, doubting that I'd even be able to do it. And I was, maybe, 10 minutes in at that point.

Then slowly, almost as if by magic, I fell into my space in the crowd. I settled into a comfortable pace, calmed down and relaxed into running. I started to regain my confidence. Everything was going to be okay. I was on track.

Having settled into the race, I soon started to think about the bigger picture and my overall strategy. I was checking my time against the distance markers, constantly assessing how I felt and whether I should adjust my pace. Go faster, maybe.

It sounds crazy now but with 90-odd kilometres ahead of me, I started thinking about the end of the race. I started thinking I should speed up, shave some time off my target finishing time. "Maybe if I do the next kilometre a bit faster, I can beat my personal best," that sort of thing. Because I felt good, I was getting too confident. I'd lost sight of the fact that it was an *ultra*-marathon, emphasis on the ultra. I still had a long way to go. What I needed to do was pace myself, hold something back now so I could dip into my reserves later. But did I?'

'I'm guessing not,' I smiled.

'You guessed right. I was feeling great. So why bother stopping at rest stops? I didn't need to fuel up and hydrate. Better to keep going and beat my target time.'

Bill shook his head in disbelief at his own folly.

'Fast-forward to midday in the race, and it was getting *hot*. The weather had thrown a total curve ball and it was unseasonably warm. That last rest stop where I didn't fill up with water suddenly felt like a very bad decision. I was thirsty and tired. And worst of all ... the hills. Where did all the hills come from? I mean, I knew it would be an undulating run, what with it being the Jurassic Coast. But these weren't hills; these were mountains. Or at least they felt like it.

One after the other, the hills kept coming. Up one side and then down the other. The downs became just as bad as the ups, sapping my strength just as much. The sun beating down relentlessly, I'd never felt so thirsty. My pace slowed to a crawl. Everything hurt. Everything. I began to doubt my ability, even question my own sanity. Why was I doing this to myself? I could just give up, call the support vehicle, and go home. I thought how nice it would be to stop moving.

It's in those tough parts of the race that you need to dig deep. You need to go back to basics, keep it simple. Instead of thinking about the finish line, you think only of the next step. You just keep putting one foot in front of the other, one step at a time. Just keep moving forward. So that's what I did.

The steps became easier. The more I focused on one step at a time, the easier I found the terrain. I stopped looking at the hill ahead and the hill after that, and thought only of each step. The afternoon moved on and the sun's heat began to dissipate. Before I knew it, the next aid station was just a few hundred metres away, then just a few metres away, then I was there. I stopped, took the time to drink and refuel.

That was a beautiful moment of mindfulness. I felt so in the moment at that rest stop. I took the time to rest, breathe, recentre. And most of all, I felt so happy that I hadn't given up. I really appreciated that rest, each mouthful of water. I was so thankful to still be there.'

'And you went on to finish the race,' I said.

Bill nodded. 'It took me over 24 hours to complete 100km. Twice as long as I had imagined. My best laid plans had been shot to hell. But I finished.

What I didn't know at the start, or even at that aid station, is that those 24 hours would be filled with a thousand little moments where I wanted to give up. A thousand moments when I thought that I couldn't go any further. A thousand times when I had to tell myself to put one foot in front of the other. Just keep moving forward. Over and over again. One step at a time.

Those 24 hours were also filled with some of the most incredible experiences of my life. Moments of pure joy and wonder. The kindness of other runners who saw me struggling and took time out of their own race to help me, cheer me along, even though they were struggling themselves. The sunrise that made me stop in my tracks and stare in awe. The rocky beach that was so painful to run on, it made us all laugh like idiots - dozens of ultramarathon runners hobbling over stones and laughing through the pain. The incredible pride I felt when I crossed the finish line and collected my medal. Once-in-a-lifetime moments.

It may have taken me twice as long to finish, but I got there in the end. And I look back now and remember those joyful moments much more than the awful moments. Even the awful moments give me a sense of satisfaction because I didn't give up. I kept putting one foot in front of the other.'

Bill sat there for a moment, holding the photograph in his hand.

'Remind you of anything?' I asked him.

THE CLIMB FROM ROCK BOTTOM IS YOUR OWN PERSONAL ULTRAMARATHON

Bill's ultramarathon experience is not unlike the climb back up from rock bottom.

You stand there on the metaphorical starting line. Your goal, the life you desire, ahead in the distance. You've done so much hard work to get to this point - you've worked through the pain of finding yourself at rock bottom. You've gathered mindset tools like gratitude and mindfulness. You've let go of fear. You're ready, confident, prepared. The path ahead is clear and full of potential. You're excited to get going on your journey towards the new you and your new life. You take your first step.

And you're off! In your excitement, you try to do too much at once. You have so many good intentions, so many changes you want to make or steps you want to take, you try and fit in too much too soon. What's more, you might be surrounded by other people with good intentions, giving you advice on what you should be doing and how to get your life back on track. Your mind is a whirl. So much conflicting advice and so many demands on your time. Can you even do this?

Letting go of the fear, you begin to settle into your journey. You relax. You're on track towards your goals. Things are going to plan. At this stage of your journey from rock bottom, you have days full of successes, peace and calm. Life is good.

This is when you might be in danger of getting over-confident, like our friend Bill skipping rest stops because he was feeling strong. Maybe you rush head-first into a new relationship without taking time to work on yourself first. Maybe you leap at opportunities that aren't quite right for you because you're desperate to get back on top. You're so focused on the end destination you forget that there's a long road ahead and the climb can't be rushed.

Then something comes along that really challenges you and tests your resolve. As it did for Bill when the midday heat set in and he hadn't taken the rest stops he needed. Maybe that opportunity you grabbed isn't working out the way you thought. Maybe that new relationship ended suddenly. You start to question your ability to achieve your goals. You might wonder why you're bothering. Maybe you should just give up. Who knew the climb would be this hard? Maybe rock bottom wasn't so bad after all...

It's at times like this - when you feel like you can't do it - when you need to focus on one step at a time. Let go of those thoughts of the finish line. Just take one more step, and another, and another. Keep moving forward and, before you know it, there will be an aid station just around the corner. That metaphorical aid station might be a small achievement, just a small win, but it'll give you a much-needed opportunity to stop, be thankful, breathe and recentre. Refuelled, you'll be ready to take the next step, and the next step after that.

Like Bill, you will reach your goal one step at a time. It may take longer than you expect and the journey may be filled with moments of doubt and exhaustion. But it will also be filled with moments of joy and gratitude. Relish those moments. When you look back, those are the moments you'll remember, much more than the not-so-fun moments.

HOW TO KEEP MOVING, ONE STEP AT A TIME

There's no magic way to reach your goal. You reach any goal by keep moving towards it. Whether it's healing from a failed relationship, regaining your health, recovering from bankruptcy, navigating redundancy and finding a new career, or whatever. One step at a time. One foot in front of the other.

It's unglamorous, I know, but that's how it's done. It's the sum of all those small steps that brings you to your goal.

And I can pretty much guarantee that things won't always go to plan. There will be bad days and setbacks. There will be times when it feels like you're not making progress, as Bill felt trying to raise funds for his charity. Sometimes you might even feel like you've taken a step backwards.

It's okay. In fact, it's normal. This is a marathon, not a sprint, and it's going to be filled with ups and downs. Which is why it's so important to concentrate on one step at a time and not worry too much about the end destination. Have faith that you'll get there, but don't focus so hard on that point in the distance. Focus instead on taking the next step.

We all know this. We all know that a marathon is made up of thousands of individual steps. But the truth is, staying focused on each step at a time is hard work. Especially when you're so keen to reach your goal.

But you have everything you need to take it one step at a time. The tools are right here in this book - your blueprint. Mindfulness will help you stay present in the moment rather than getting overwhelmed by the future. Gratitude will help you stay grounded and positive, even when things don't go to plan. Meditation and deep breathing does wonders in moments of stress and doubt. Affirmations will remind you that you *can* do it. Taking care of your physical and mental self will give you strength. Creating a routine of positive habits will help you stay committed to the journey. Use these tools over and over again on your climb.

And yes, you may need to accept losses and failures along the way. That's also fine. Remember, it's part of striving for things and moving forwards.

Finally, you'll want to find ways to stay connected to the bigger picture - the thing you're working towards - *without focusing too hard on it*. A way of keeping your goals in your heart and mind, without losing sight of the step right in front of you. Basically, you want to feel motivated to take that next step, without feeling daunted by all the steps to come after that. As you'll see in the next chapter, I have a few more mindset tools up my sleeve to help you stay excited about your end goal.

LESSONS FROM THE CLIMB

- It's the sum of many small steps that will bring you to your goal. Your climb from rock bottom is a marathon, not a sprint. Sometimes it may even feel like an ultramarathon!
- It's normal to have times when you feel like you're no longer making progress, or things are moving too slowly. It's normal to have moments of doubt.
- At times like these you need to just put one foot in front of the other. Stop focusing on the final goal and think only of the next step. One step at a time. One day at a time.
- The mindset tools we've covered so far in this book - tools like mindfulness and gratitude - will help you stay in the moment and avoid getting overwhelmed by the bigger picture.
- Taking it one step at a time can be hard. But you will get there. You will reach your goal so long as you keep moving towards it, step by step.

Let's delve into this concept of keeping faith in the bigger picture without getting overwhelmed by it. In the next chapter, we'll explore some additional mindset approaches that will motivate you to keep moving forward, one step at a time.

Chapter 10

HARNESSING THE POWER OF MINDSET

Bill read me the message on his phone, 'I don't think we're a good fit, but it was nice getting to know you. I wish you all the best. Take care.'

'Oooof,' I said. 'Pretty clear cut. So what did you say back?'

Bill sighed. 'What could I say? I said I was disappointed but that I wished her all the best, too. I tried to sound casual about it, but to be honest, I was totally blindsided. We'd had six dates. I thought things were going really well. I couldn't believe it when she sent me this last week.'

'That sucks. I'm sorry. Dating can be hard.'

'Hard?' Bill said. 'More like impossible. Between the day job, the weekend job, having Callie half the time, and all the admin that comes with being on these dating apps ... I don't know how people keep this up for months or years at a time. It's exhausting. I just want to meet someone nice to share time with. I'm not asking for much.'

BILL HITS A BUMP IN THE ROAD

We've fast-forwarded several months in Bill's journey. His non-profit aimed at helping men heal through nature was up and running – as a side hustle for now. Bill was working four days a week in his corporate job and running excursions and events a couple of weekends a month, when his daughter was at her mum's. But it was off the ground and making progress. Bill had managed to secure a bit of funding from local organisations, the early feedback from clients was really positive, and best of all, Bill felt an enormous sense of satisfaction from the work. Spending time in nature, helping people connect with their surroundings, allowing them to be in the moment and learn new skills ... it was everything Bill hoped it would be. It was a small start, but it was going well. His daughter was proud of him. Life was good.

So good that Bill had decided to dip his toes into the dating pool. He wasn't looking for anything very serious, but he felt ready to date.

He'd had a couple of 'alright' first dates – nothing disastrous but not enough of a connection to warrant a second date. Then he met Kate. They seemed to hit it off well and had enjoyed half a dozen dates. It wasn't love. At least, not yet. But Bill certainly thought they had potential.

Her message ending the relationship had come out of the blue. And I could tell Bill was gutted.

'She must have met someone else,' he said, still looking at the message. 'Someone she liked more.'

'Maybe,' I said, carefully. 'It happens. You'll probably never know. But hey, it's all part of the process, right? Just because this relationship didn't work out doesn't mean the next one won't.'

The phone in Bill's hand started ringing.

He looked at the name on the screen and tutted. 'Ugh, what does she want now?' he said. He answered the phone and walked away.

From the snippets of conversation I overheard, it was clear that Bill was talking to his ex-wife. After a brief but tense discussion, Bill concluded with an angry, 'Fine. Whatever.' He hung up, muttering to himself as he walked back to me.

'What was that all about?' I asked.

'Just Callie's gymnastics tournament tomorrow.' Bill answered. 'She wanted to check I'd remembered.'

'Oh,' I said. 'Only it sounded kind of heated...'

Bill sighed again. 'That's how all of our conversations seem to go lately. Especially since this thing with Kate last week. I see my ex-wife's name come up on the screen and I just get this overwhelming wave of anger and resentment. Even the most basic conversation ends up in an argument.'

'Is this even about your wife, though?' I asked. 'Or is it about someone you went on a few dates with?'

Bill thought for a second. 'I mean, both. Being dumped suddenly. Again. It's brought it all back. All the pain and abandonment of the divorce. I thought I was in a good place. I *was* in a good place. But now I just feel so angry all over again.'

'You did sound kind of defensive,' I said, gently.

'I know,' Bill admitted. 'I just can't seem to help myself. I want us to have this civil, respectful relationship. For Callie's sake, you know. But then I'm abrupt and defensive, and then so is she, and we end up getting into the stupidest arguments. I don't know how to break the cycle.'

'You could stop letting your thoughts and feelings dictate your actions,' I said. 'It's natural to feel angry and hurt at times. But you can decide how you respond.'

'Except I can't seem to,' Bill said.

'What you need is a buffer.'

CHOOSING YOUR RESPONSE TO SITUATIONS

'A buffer?' Bill asked.

'Yeah,' I continued. 'You know that quote, "Between stimulus and response, there is a space?"'

'I've not heard it,' Bill said.

'It's by Holocaust survivor Victor Frankl. He said in that space, the space between stimulus and response, lies our freedom and power to choose our response. And in our response, lies our growth and happiness.'

'Powerful stuff,' Bill said.

'In other words,' I replied, 'when you think a thought or feel a feeling, you can recognise that stimulus for what it is - as in, it's just a thought or a feeling. That's all. And then you can choose your actions in response.'

'Except, what if I don't feel much of a space between the thought, feeling and response? That's what I'm struggling with.'

I nodded. 'But that's where you pull on tools like meditation. Regular meditation or mindfulness can reduce your overall feelings of stress and anger - so you're better able to respond in the moment. Even just taking a deep breath before you answer the phone creates a buffer. One simple deep breath or a count to three can create a buffer between your thoughts, feelings and actions.'

'I guess.' Bill didn't sound totally convinced.

I continued, 'You could also try affirmations as a way to create a buffer or change the way you feel. You could say something like, "I choose to respond from a place of calmness," or "I co-parent well." Use it as a buffer before you respond. And remember, in your response lies your happiness and growth.'

'Okay...' Bill still sounded unconvinced.

'Think of it this way,' I said, 'how is your response making you feel at the moment?'

'Pretty shitty.'

'Exactly. And the shittier you feel about it, the more likely you are to attract more shitty feelings, more shitty conversations. Like attracts like, after all. You're a magnet.'

THE LAW OF ATTRACTION AND THE IDEA THAT 'LIKE ATTRACTS LIKE'

'Oh God, you're talking about *The Secret*?' Bill asked. 'That book from a few years ago?'

'That book changed my life,' I said. 'No exaggeration. That book, the whole idea of the law of attraction, taught me that I attract things to me by my thoughts and feelings. Good thoughts and feelings attract more good things my way, and negative thoughts and feelings attract negative things my way. If I'm in a crappy mood and I don't do anything to shake it off, I only end up attracting more crappy things. Same sort of thing with you. Your response to this situation is only attracting more tense conversations with your ex.'

'You're saying I'm a crap magnet,' Bill said.

I laughed. 'Well, I'm saying that you attract back what you put out there – good or bad. That's the basic idea, anyway. You should read the book. It gave me a really practical way to master my thoughts. As the law of attraction says, thoughts create feelings, and feelings create actions. Thoughts become things. Therefore, if you use the law of attraction to take control of your thoughts, you *create* better things around you. You manifest the things you want instead of the things you don't want.'

'But how?' Bill asked.

'Like, when I was really struggling financially, back after the financial crisis. I could have thought about negative things like debt, or being broke, or the investments I'd lost. But the law of attraction taught me that focusing on the things you lack means you'll only attract more scarcity your way. Whereas if you focus on abundance, you'll attract abundance. So even though I was broke, I focused my mind on thoughts of prosperity and wealth, not debt and poverty, or the fact that I only had enough money in the bank to live from month to month. I focused on wealth, success, and an incredible life – and that's what I attracted.'

'But, like, *how*?' Bill asked. 'How exactly did you take control of your thoughts?'

'It's nothing you don't already know,' I said. 'I set goals that motivated me. I used affirmations to create positive thoughts and feelings. I took care of my physical and mental health to help me maintain a more positive attitude. I used gratitude to focus on abundance rather than the things I lacked. I used meditation and mindfulness to help me react from a place of calm. These all feed into the law of attraction and help me manifest the things I want. But one of the best law of attraction tools is visualisation.'

VISUALISATION AS A WAY TO HARNESS THE LAW OF ATTRACTION

'That's a new one,' Bill said.

'I use visualisation all the time as a way to focus on the things I want to happen, rather than the things I don't want to happen. Just by creating vivid mental pictures of the things I want - daydreaming, in a way - I can stay focused on my goals and help manifest them. It also helps me shape my thoughts, feelings and actions. Which could be really useful for you right now.'

'How so?' Bill asked.

I explained, 'So, you can use visualisation for your bigger-picture goals. That's how many people use visualisation. But you can also use it to shift your thoughts and feelings to a more positive place - and, in turn, manifest a better relationship with your ex. Why not try visualising a situation where you and your ex have built that civil, respectful relationship you want? You could imagine the two of you at Callie's graduation, feeling proud of the person you created and enjoying that special moment together. Imagine the two of you having a friendly conversation and speaking to each other warmly. Imagine a super-specific scenario and conjure up the feelings that come with that scenario. Keep doing it, over and over again. Begin to think, speak and act as though that scenario has come true. I promise it'll help.'

DID IT WORK?

The next time I checked in with Bill, he'd read *The Secret* and was learning to use the law of attraction and visualisation to his advantage. His relationship with his ex-wife was getting better by the week. Everything felt de-escalated. Bill was even ready to try dating again – without linking his dating successes or failures back to his marriage. He felt more in control of his thoughts, feelings and actions.

'When the phone rings, or I get a message from my ex, I don't automatically think perfect thoughts,' Bill confessed to me. 'I'm not an angel. I'm still hurt. But I recognise the thoughts for what they are and I recognise how they make me feel. I remind myself that thoughts can be changed, and that I'm in control of how I respond to my feelings. Basically, I tell myself that I decide my actions, so how can I act in a way that creates a more constructive conversation?'

'That's amazing,' I said.

'And the more I do things like meditate, or use affirmations, or visualise us having totally normal conversations, the easier it gets. The more in control I feel. We even had a coffee together when she dropped Callie off yesterday. A few months ago, even a few weeks ago, I never would have imagined us getting to that place.'

'See? You're manifesting exactly what you want. And you can use this technique for all sorts of things, big and small, short term and long term.'

TAKING CONTROL OF YOUR THOUGHTS AND FEELINGS

Most people believe that thoughts and feelings are just to be accepted for what they are -uncontrollable. Be honest, how many times have you said something like, 'I can't help how I feel'?

But you *can* help how you think and feel. By declaring that your thoughts and feelings are uncontrollable, you give away your power. Your power to act in ways you want. Your power to go after the things you desire. Your power to live life your way.

The law of attraction is all about mastering your thoughts and feelings in order to manifest the life you want. Because you can learn to *choose* your thoughts, consciously. Just as you'd choose which socks to put on, or which film to watch on a Friday night. And in turn, those thoughts create your feelings.

Your mindset is your biggest asset in the climb from rock bottom. At times, you may feel like you're in a battle with your mind. There will be times when you feel doubt, or fear, or frustration. But with the right mindset tools, you can take charge of your thoughts and feelings, instead of giving your power away.

Everything we've talked about so far in this book - meditation, positive affirmations, gratitude, etc. - will help you harness the power of your mind. But now it's time for us to delve into one of the most impactful mindset tools you can have in your toolbox: the law of attraction.

Why wait until now to talk about the law of attraction? Because I've found it useful on two particular fronts. Firstly, the law of attraction helps me stay connected to my goals and think in a way that supports my goals. Which makes it a great tool to have up your sleeve as you tackle your climb from rock bottom. Basically, it can help you stay connected to the bigger picture of your journey, and have faith that you will achieve the life you desire, without getting overwhelmed by the *hows* and *whens* of it all.

Which in turn allows you to take things one step at a time, confidently, knowing you will get there.

And secondly, when I hit bumps in the road - any sort of bump - the law of attraction gives me a way to tune my thoughts and feelings to a more positive frequency. Again, this can be an extremely helpful tool at any point on your journey from rock bottom.

But what exactly is the law of attraction and how can you use it? Let's get into it.

A QUICK PRIMER ON THE LAW OF ATTRACTION

Like attracts like. Thoughts become things. What you think about, comes about. Where attention goes, energy flows.

These are some of the core principles of the law of attraction - a universal law that says we create the world around us with our thoughts and feelings. It was popularised in the bestselling book *The Secret* but even if you haven't read the book, I bet you can recognise what I'm talking about.

For example, think about a certain type of car, or a certain holiday destination and - bam! - I bet you start seeing or hearing about it everywhere you go. Or let's say you wake up in a foul mood one day and spend your morning snapping at everyone. What is the result? More things go wrong. Every traffic light turns red as you approach. People seem extra rude. The whole world seems against you.

According to the law of attraction, you are a magnet. Your thoughts emit a powerful magnetic force that attracts the things that you think about most. Good or bad.

It's common sense, really. If you're in a bad mood, you're bound to notice more negative things around you. But that doesn't make the law of attraction any less powerful. When harnessed properly and used as a tool for achieving the things you want, the law of attraction delivers incredible results. It has for me. And it works across all areas of life: transforming your thoughts, attitude and behaviour; building a dream career; achieving wealth and prosperity; living a healthy life; finding love, you name it.

The law of attraction is about manifesting the things you most want out of life - providing you use it properly. Because you can also manifest the things you *don't* want. Have you ever really focused on something you didn't want, with all your might, and then that very thing ended up happening? It could be something small like 'I don't want to get sick on holiday' or it could be something major like 'I don't want to get into more debt.' It's an example of how our thoughts create the things around us. Not by magic, but because our thoughts create feelings and feelings create actions. So by focusing only on debt (as opposed to wealth and abundance) you act with thoughts of debt (rather than prosperity) in mind.

When I lost almost everything after the financial crash, if I had continued to focus on all the things I *didn't* have, on everything I'd lost, and how broke I was, I'm certain I wouldn't be where I am today. But instead, I thought of myself as successful and fortunate and, yes, wealthy - even though my bank balance said otherwise.

That's not to say every bad thought you have will bring about disaster. Of course it won't. We all have negative thoughts from time to time. The law of attraction isn't about policing every little thought that pops into your head. That way lies madness! Rather, it's about your overall pattern of thought. So if your pattern of thought generally tends towards the good things in life, the wonderful things you already have (big and small), and the bright future ahead, that's what you will manifest. But if you overwhelmingly think that everything will go wrong, that you'll be a terrible failure and never achieve anything with your life - well, that's probably what will happen. At least according to the law of attraction.

As Henry Ford put it, 'Whether you think you can or you think you can't, you're right.'

USING THE LAW OF ATTRACTION

So how can you use the law of attraction to your advantage? Well, the simplest thing you can do is retune your overall pattern of thought to be more positive. And everything we've talked about so far in this book will help you do that. Things like meditation, gratitude, and so on.

You can also surround yourself with more positive people. People who generally look on the bright side of life and lift up those around them, as opposed to people who constantly drag others down. We'll talk more about finding your people in Chapter 11.

You can also check in with your feelings on a regular basis. Because remember, your thoughts create your feelings. So rather than policing every little thought that pops into your head, just tap into your feelings at several times across the day. If you're feeling relaxed, that's a pretty good sign that your underlying thoughts are generally positive. Feeling tense, sad or anxious? Your underlying thoughts have probably slipped into negative territory.

I find this gives me a quick indication of how my brain is working, without having to analyse every little thought. And if I notice that I'm not feeling so great, I do something to shift my thoughts and feelings. Maybe a little gratitude. Maybe a positive affirmation or two. Or maybe I'll pop on a song that makes me want to dance stupidly.

ASK, BELIEVE, RECEIVE

I highly recommend you read *The Secret*. It's a quick read and very inspirational. (There's a film version if that's more up your street. There's even an app to help you put the law of attraction into practice.) In the book, author Rhonda Byrne sets out three steps to help you use the law of attraction as a practical tool:

- Step 1 is Ask. This is all about setting goals and defining what you want in life so that you can focus your thoughts accordingly. In other words, don't think about the things you *don't* want – send your attention towards the things you *do* want. Thoughts become things. What you think about comes about.
- Step 2 is Believe. Trust that the things you want will be yours. Cultivate a feeling of certainty that everything you want is coming your way and relax into that certainty. Think, speak and act from this place of certainty. Positive affirmations are really useful for this. As is visualisation – but we'll talk more about visualisation in a bit.
- Step 3 is Receive. This last step is all about feeling good. Feel the way you'll feel when you achieve the life you desire. Feel those feelings now. The feelings of being happy, loved, successful, content, healthy, wealthy ... or whatever else you want in life. Feel those amazing feelings of joy, satisfaction, and gratitude, and let it supercharge your belief. Visualisation is especially helpful here.

Steps two and three can take a little practice, especially if life hasn't gone your way lately. It can be hard to believe that the universe is *for* you, not against you. But once you conjure up that feeling of belief and begin to live as if you've already achieved the life you desire, it's utterly transformative. There's something so freeing about letting go, and trusting that the universe will deliver.

That's not to say you never have to do anything to achieve your goals. You must keep working towards your goals, whatever they are, one step at a time. But it's a wonderful feeling to know that, as you move closer to the things you want, the universe is also bringing them a step closer. Because your thoughts, feelings and actions are creating the world around you. All the time.

DAYDREAMING YOUR GOALS INTO EXISTENCE – THE POWER OF VISUALISATION

Visualisation is a great way to take control of your thoughts, and focus your mindset on the things you want. As such it's a practical way to put the law of attraction into action.

Is it really just daydreaming? Well, yes and no. Think of it as a more structured form of daydreaming. Instead of just letting your mind wander wherever it fancies, visualisation means directing your imagination towards a specific mental picture that's related to your goal or goals.

In this way, visualisation is a fantastic tool that supports your goals - helping you stay confident that you will get where you want to go. But it's also a really useful mental health tool to pull out of the bag whenever negativity, doubt or worry creeps in - and that goes for whether you're nervous about a work presentation, scared of going on a first date, or anxious about your health.

In fact, medical studies have found visualisation can have very real physical benefits, not just mental. It's been proven to speed recovery, helping patients recover from surgery faster than patients who don't use visualisation. And it has been shown to help athletes recover from injury faster. Why? It's probably because visualisation lowers stress (which has been shown to hinder healing), and enhances feelings of calmness and positivity. I have absolutely found that visualisation lowers my stress levels and makes me feel more positive. It's therefore a great tool to use alongside meditation and mindfulness - or if you don't feel like meditation is for you, perhaps visualisation is more up your street.

Personally, I've also found that visualisation helps to enhance my concentration. Whether I'm picturing a big life goal or a small scenario like a successful meeting at work, I feel more focused after a brief visualisation exercise.

Visualisation is, at heart, a form of creative thinking – and I think that's a big part of why visualisation is so powerful. Creative thinking is an important predictor of success (both academic success and life success). In fact, some experts believe creativity may be a bigger predictor of success than intelligence. In other words, by tapping into your imagination, you're sowing the seeds for success. I don't know about you, but I love that.

Let's explore how you can use visualisation to support your goals and enhance your wellbeing.

WHAT SORTS OF THINGS CAN YOU VISUALISE?

Whatever you want, really. A huge life goal. A smaller, short-term goal. A specific situation that you'd like to go well.

Anything goes, then. But I will say that visualisation is at its most powerful when you focus on specific goals, scenarios or outcomes, rather than general wishes like 'I want to feel free'. So rather than just wishing for 'freedom', define what that looks like to you. For example, you might picture yourself shutting your laptop down at 3pm, walking out into your beautiful garden, and enjoying an iced coffee in your hammock – because you have the freedom to set your own hours and work whenever you want.

Don't have a beautiful garden and hammock? Doesn't matter! Your visualisation doesn't have to be tied to your real life as it is now. It's not an exercise in realism; it's an exercise in creative thinking. So if part of your ideal future life includes a beautiful new house and garden, work that into your visualisation.

The key, then, is to define what you want to achieve (so, refer back to your goals, as per Chapter 6), and use visualisation as a tool to help bring those goals to life. As the law of attraction says, where attention goes energy flows. So by focusing your creative attention on the things that you want to achieve, you manifest those goals. You bring them to life.

I know that this works because I've manifested lots of goals through the law of attraction and visualisation. I've manifested my dream sports car (when I was a younger man, that is, pe-children - although I must confess, I'm still a car nut). I've manifested a beautiful family life. I've manifested growth in my business. I've manifested my goal of presenting on television. Because I visualised these scenarios with all my might and breathed life into them.

Your own scenarios can be anything you want. In fact, what I love about visualisation is it can be used to breathe life into literally any kind of goal.

What's more, you can use visualisation to picture one-off scenarios going well. If my children are nervous about something at school, for example, I encourage them to visualise it going brilliantly. (In this way, visualisation is an excellent technique to use in preparation for a high-stress situation, like an important meeting, an exam, or whatever.) Same thing with my friend Bill wanting to have better, more constructive conversations with his ex-wife - by visualising it happening, he could think, speak and act in line with that goal.

Visualisation can therefore help you change your behaviour, and even build new habits - as well as achieve the life you desire. I mentioned before that I've always been scared of public speaking. So I use visualisation as a tool to help me overcome that. By picturing myself doing a good job in front of the camera, or making a presentation, I'm reprogramming my mind. I start to think and act like someone who is a confident public speaker. It works.

HOW TO VISUALISE

The first step is to define what you want to visualise. So at this point you may look at your goal list or dream board as a reminder (in fact, the dream board serves as a brilliant prompt for visualisation exercises because it's already in a visual format). Or you may simply decide on a smaller goal or scenario that you want to imagine. Remember, don't focus on general wishes or desires - visualisation is at its most powerful when applied to concrete goals, situations and outcomes. It works best when your daydream is super-specific and detailed.

Want to find a loving relationship, for example? Visualise yourself on a Sunday morning stroll, holding hands with your loved one as you walk your dog together. Picture the beautiful place where you're walking and the smell of fresh air. Imagine the feel of your partner's hand in yours. Imagine their face, even. Imagine the beautiful softness of their eyes as they smile at you. Feel that feeling of being loved.

Or let's say you want to start your own bakery. Visualise that space and be as detailed as possible. What colour are the walls? What apron are you wearing? How does the worktop feel under your hand? Imagine that smell of fresh bread and coffee. (It's making me hungry as I write this!) Picture the smile on your face as you greet regular customers. Picture the sun streaming in the window and the cute little table and chairs outside. Imagine it all and feel the feeling of satisfaction that comes from creating the business of your dreams.

And if you want to visualise a smaller scenario, like a job interview, simply imagine that scenario going well. Picture yourself looking sharp and feeling confident. Visualise yourself speaking in a fluid, self-assured way. You smile at the interviewer and take a relaxed sip of water. You already feel at home in this organisation. You feel a rapport with this person who will be your boss. They respond to you with warmth. They want you on their team!

Whether you're picturing a big or small goal, try following this basic pattern of visualisation:

- Create a vivid and rich mental image of achieving the thing you want.

- Tap into the positive feelings that go along with achieving that goal. Really feel those feelings of excitement, pride and gratitude.
- Settle into a feeling of certainty. You will manifest this scenario. It is coming.

That last point is crucial. The biggest piece of visualisation advice I give anyone is to *believe*. Believe in what you're visualising. Attach a sense of calm certainty to your goals. You need to believe it will happen. If you don't, you completely undermine the exercise.

Here's an example of how I put these steps into practice. At the time of writing, my family and I are waiting to get the keys to our new home. This has been a long time coming and we've made several temporary house moves in the last few months as we wait for this new property to be ready. With three children, it's been a stressful time for our family. Visualising us taking ownership of the new house has, at times, kept me sane! Here's how I do it:

I settle into a comfy seat. It's early morning and the kids are still asleep. Everything is peaceful. I have a few minutes to myself.

I pull up a picture of our new house on my phone. Then I close my eyes.

I imagine I'm holding the keys to the house. I imagine the weight of the keys in my hand and the tinkle of metal as I shake the keys in celebration. We're all so excited to step inside.

I open the door and the kids rush past me into the house, squealing with excitement. As I listen to the stomps of their feet rushing up the stairs, I take in the smell of the house - there's the faintest smell of fresh paint.

I can see through the open-plan downstairs towards the beautiful back garden. My wife opens the folding doors and we stand together on the flagstone patio, my arm around her, the smooth stones under my feet. The birds are singing and I can smell the nearby pine trees.

'It's ours,' I say to my wife.

'Time to celebrate,' she says.

I watch my wife as she goes back into the kitchen. On the marble worktop, she sets down the cooler box we packed for this special occasion. She opens it and pulls out the bottle of champagne and two plastic cups. She brings them to the patio, I open the bottle and pour us two glasses of bubbly.

I tap into the emotions I feel at us embarking on this new phase of our life. I feel proud and thankful. I feel excited to host family and friends here. I'm smiling in my vision, and in real life, as the emotions wash over me. The sensation of joy is so strong I feel almost on the verge of tears.

Finally, I let a feeling of certainty settle over me. Certainty that this vision will come to life, soon. I let that feeling reassure and calm me.

I sit in silence for a few minutes, holding this vivid picture in my mind and enjoying the sensations that go with it.

I often experience intense positive emotions while visualising. Give it a try yourself, and I bet you'll be surprised at the powerful feelings that are unleashed. And the great news is, those positive feelings stay with me throughout the day. You don't have to visualise in the morning, as I do, but I will say it's an amazing way to start the day.

Whenever and wherever you visualise, regular practice is key. So try to get into the habit of visualising on a regular basis - ideally daily, but a few times a week is better than nothing.

HOW **NOT** TO VISUALISE

Visualisation is a powerful force for good if you use it to imagine *positive* scenarios and outcomes. It's about filling your brain with images of a bright future - and picturing everything that can and will go right. So don't picture the things you don't want to happen or imagine things going wrong.

Let's take the bakery example. Your mind could easily wander to all the obstacles that stand in your way. How can you afford to quit your job? How will you fund the business? Are you even a good enough baker? Remember what the law of attraction says - we get what we think about most. So imagine yourself running that successful bakery.

And yes, I understand that visualising the positives instead of the negatives doesn't come naturally to everyone. I've had those moments where my brain automatically goes straight for the worst possible outcome. But remember what we said at the start of this chapter - thoughts can always be changed. You can, quite simply, decide to think differently. Create a buffer if you need to, by taking a mindful moment or a deep breath. Then send that negative thought on its way and choose your next thought.

Another potential pitfall with visualisation is thinking it's a substitute for taking action. It's not. Visualisation is a powerful tool, but you still have to take practical steps and stay open to opportunities that will bring you closer to your goals, one step at a time.

LESSONS FROM THE CLIMB

- Your mind is your greatest asset on the climb from rock bottom. But you need to learn how to master it. How to respond to negative thoughts and feelings. And how to tune your mind to more positive thoughts.
- Between stimulus and response lies a space. And in that space you have the power to choose your response. In other words, you can recognise thoughts and feelings for what they are and choose how you act. Tools like meditation, mindfulness, and affirmations can help you change your thoughts or feelings - or simply create a brief buffer between the thought and your response to it.

- The law of attraction says that our thoughts and feelings create the world around us. We attract the things we think about most, good or bad. We get back what we put out there, basically.
- The law of attraction is about taking control of your thoughts and feelings, in order to manifest the life you want. *The Secret* sets out a three-step process for this: ask, believe, receive. Ask for the things you want and define your goals. Believe with all your heart that you will achieve the life you desire. And feel good, as if you have already received everything you want.
- Visualisation is a great way to take charge of your thoughts and focus your energy on the things you want to manifest in life – big or small. Visualisation also has proven physical benefits.
- Visualisation is at its most powerful when you focus on specific goals or outcomes, rather than general wishes. Create a super-specific scenario in your head, including sights, sounds and sensations. Feel the accompanying feelings of joy and satisfaction and gratitude. And settle into a feeling of certainty that your vision will come to life.
- Visualisation can even help you change your behaviours and build positive habits – by imagining yourself living those behaviours and habits.

Visualisation and the law of attraction can be massive motivation-boosters. They've certainly helped me stay committed to my goals and feel excited about the things I'm working towards. But let's explore some other tips for staying motivated on your climb from rock bottom.

Chapter 11

STAYING MOTIVATED
(HINT: IT'S ABOUT PEOPLE)

I'd noticed a distinct change in Bill in recent months. He seemed more open. Especially open to new people.

You know those people who are always the centre of attention at a party? That person who's bang smack in the middle of a crowd, telling a raucous story, holding everyone's attention, perfectly comfortable among friends and strangers alike?

My friend Bill was *not* that person. Bill was active, outdoorsy and liked to laugh. But I'd never describe him as a 'people person' or extrovert. He had a small circle of friends and maintained close connections with those people, but he didn't bring new people into the fold easily. He was at his happiest sharing a quiet beer in the garden or dragging his daughter on a walk.

So I'd been pretty surprised when Bill first mentioned the idea of setting up a charity working with groups of men at a time. Heading off on camping and hiking trips with people he didn't know. I mean, it was a brilliant idea. But a very un-Bill thing to do.

And talking about his feelings? Until his marriage broke down, Bill had never spoken in any deep way about how he was feeling. To me, to a therapist, or to anyone as far as I knew.

He wasn't the type of person to say if he was struggling or sad or anxious. That just wasn't Bill. Except, now it was. Bill had recognised pretty quickly when he hit rock bottom that 'going it alone' wasn't going to work this time, and he needed extra reinforcements. That's what led him to talk to me, and then a therapist.

And now, more than a year down the line, I noticed Bill would speak much more freely about how he was feeling - with me and other friends, even with his daughter. Bill had always been more of the 'strong and silent' type of dad. But now, he was comfortable saying to his daughter that he was feeling nervous about a date, or feeling proud of the work his charity was doing. He was comfortable opening up.

The change in Bill really hit home when I came along on one of his charity's events - a foraging hike, organised with a local mushroom and wild food expert. Bill was so at home with this small group of strangers, talking about his childhood picking mushrooms with his grandad. He knew when to open up about his experience of getting divorced and how nature had helped him. And he knew when to create space for others to share their feelings.

I was in awe of Bill's growth.

THE IMPORTANCE OF OPENING YOURSELF UP TO OTHERS

After the group had returned to the carpark on the edge of the woodland, I had a few moments with Bill.

'She's great,' I said, referring to the foraging expert who had helped Bill lead the hike. 'She really knows her mushrooms.'

'Amazing, isn't she?' Bill said. 'I'm so glad she agreed to give some time to this project. I think it went really well today.'

'Definitely. How did you meet?'

'We both volunteered on one of the local beach cleanup afternoons. And then I signed up for one of her courses. I'm doing another one next month on cooking with wild foods. As soon as this project starts bringing in more money, I thought we could organise retreats together where we forage and cook all our own food.'

'Sounds amazing. So she's going to be more involved in future?' I asked.

'I hope so, as soon as I can afford to pay her for her time. For now, she's doing this on a voluntary basis. I've also connected with a forester who does traditional woodcraft. He's interested in running a few workshops with me.'

I was impressed. 'Sounds like it's quite a team effort.'

'Tell me about it!' Bill said. 'I'm also hiring a virtual PA to help me get more organised. I can't do everything myself. I don't *want* to do everything myself.'

I smiled and shook my head.

'What?' Bill asked.

'Nothing ... it's just this is quite a change from the Bill of old. Look at you gathering people around you. Allowing others to help you. Talking about how you feel. Inspiring people. I'm really proud.'

Bill smiled. 'Well, one of the best things to come out of this past year is realising I need to open myself up to people. Surround myself with people who can support me and keep me going - in a practical way, and an emotional way.'

'So you're still seeing the therapist then?' I asked.

'Every other week. Making that first appointment with a therapist was the best decision I ever made. She helped keep me on track in those early days. She still stops me spiralling when I have the odd wobble. And I guess I've just adopted that collaborative approach in other areas of life - like finding good people who can help me grow this charity. People who know things I don't know and can motivate me to keep moving forward.'

BUILDING A SUPPORT NETWORK

He poured me a tea from his flask and we perched on the edge of his car boot.

'It's funny,' Bill continued. 'The more I open up to other people, the more support and love comes back to me. I didn't expect that. I always closed myself off because I didn't want to drag others down or seem weak. But that's not been the case at all. I felt so lonely in those early days of the split. If I'm honest, I felt lonely before the split. But now I feel more supported than ever. I've got my therapist, my friends. I'm making new friends. I'm connecting with others through this charity. I feel seen, if that makes sense.'

'Makes total sense,' I said. 'You're finding your people.'

'Yes!' Bill said. 'That's exactly how it feels.'

I smiled. 'It's that law of attraction magic at work. You're a magnet. By opening yourself up to others, by showing up and not closing yourself off – other people show up for you.'

'Speaking of needing others... I need your help with something. The next step after finding a virtual PA is to find a business mentor. It's been so long since I ran my first business, I need someone who can guide me as I try to grow this organisation – turn it from a side gig into my full-time job. Did you have a business mentor when you were starting out?'

'I wish,' I said. 'Finding a mentor who specialised in property strategies was near-on impossible back then. We're talking nearly 20 years ago. It's different now, obviously. But I wish I'd had someone I could learn from on a one-on-one basis. That's partly why I run the property mentorship programmes now, to give people the leg up that I didn't have.'

Bill shook his head. 'Okay, no worries. I'm sure I can find someone.'

'Look, I know I'm not an expert on any of this nature stuff, or running a non-profit, but I'd be happy to help guide you in other ways, if you like. Juggling the demands of running your own business, looking for investors, networking tips, that sort of thing.'

'I'd like that,' Bill said.

'Obviously you might want to work with more than one mentor - like you said, someone with experience of growing a non-profit. I'm sure there are networking events that specialise in non-profits.'

'There are in London,' Bill said. 'I've pencilled in a few.'

'Blimey,' I said. 'Networking, volunteering to clear up the local beach, expanding your circle. It's a whole new Bill.'

'Oh, shut up,' Bill said. But his smile said he was proud of himself.

'If I may make another suggestion,' I said, 'you might also want to work with a life coach.'

'But I already have a therapist. Isn't it basically the same thing?' Bill asked.

'Mmmm, similar, in that they can both help you improve your wellbeing. But a life coach will also help you improve your overall quality of life. You know, staying motivated, being inspired, how to achieve the things you want, boost your career, and so on. I'd say a life coach is more forward-looking, whereas a therapist helps you make sense of the past and present. So both are useful. You said that signing up for therapy was the best decision you made. I feel a similar way about working with a life coach. Most of the mindset tools I know, I learned from her. She helped me set new goals for myself and level up my business. I went from feeling slightly stagnated and frustrated to supercharging my career - and I put a lot of that down to working with a life coach. Anyway, give it some thought.'

'I will,' Bill nodded.

I gave him a final piece of advice. 'Remember, your support network isn't just for practical help and emotional support. You also need people who can fill your inspiration cup.'

FINDING YOUR PEOPLE

The climb up from rock bottom can be hard. There will be days when you feel like curling up under the covers and going back to sleep. Days when you just want to say, 'Nope'. These are the days when your motivation is at its lowest. To ensure these days are in the minority - that you have more good days than bad days - you need strategies to keep your motivation up. Ways to keep moving forward when the temptation is to stay still, stop, or even give up.

So why have I talked so much about other people in this chapter?

Because the people around you make all the difference to your motivation.

Bill found that creating his own support network was crucial to his climb from rock bottom. Friends and family, mentors, colleagues, a therapist, life coach, or even a virtual PA to take on some of the admin burden ... these are the sorts of people that will help you keep your spirits up, remain focused on what you want, and stay motivated.

I wanted to devote a whole chapter to this because, no doubt about it, rock bottom can be a lonely place. It can be difficult to admit to those around you that you're struggling, or that you're embarking on a journey of self-improvement. Which is why so many people at rock bottom isolate themselves from others. It's easier than admitting that you're scared, sad, in pain, vulnerable...

But as the law of attraction teaches us, you get back what you put out there. If you close yourself off to others, people will close themselves off from you. Whereas if you put yourself out there and open yourself up, you'll be amazed at the support and love that flows back to you.

If rock bottom caused you to cut yourself off from others, take this as a huge neon sign to reverse that decision. Now is exactly when you should be opening up to others. Now's the time to build or reinforce your support network. Because bringing others along with you is a great way to stay motivated. It's arguably *the* best way to stay motivated. (But don't worry, we'll also cover other tips later in the chapter.)

So how can you find your people - the people who will guide and support you along the way? Let's find out.

TAPPING INTO EMOTIONAL SUPPORT

Part of your support network should include people you can turn to for emotional support. Or even just a friendly shoulder to cry on from time to time.

For many of us, friends and family meet this need. But not everyone has loved ones they can turn to - and even if they do, not everyone is comfortable sharing their innermost thoughts with the people who know them best.

I will say if you do have friends and family you can turn to, don't shut them out on your climb from rock bottom. I understand the temptation to insulate them from what's going on. I get you don't want to freak them out. But as Bill found, opening up to loved ones isn't weak. It can be incredibly healing.

If you can't or don't want to turn to friends and family, I urge you to connect with a therapist or charity that can meet your needs - whether it's a mental health charity, a support group of some kind, or whatever.

You might also want to consider volunteering for local organisations as a way to increase your social circle. I've certainly found that giving back and helping others has given me a mental boost when I need it most, but we'll talk more about that in the next chapter.

FILLING YOUR INSPIRATIONAL CUP

As I said to Bill, your support network isn't just about people who can give you emotional support - it's also about finding people who inspire you and nudge you to be your best.

Inspiration may come in the form of a mentorship relationship, a life coach, networking with other people, or simply reading books by successful people (and/or following them on social media) and gleaning tips from their journey. That's right, the person who inspires you the most might be someone you've never met in real life but have followed from afar.

When I was on my journey from rock bottom, I hoovered up so many success-building habits, traits and techniques just from reading books about what other successful people do. This motivated me to do better, to keep going on the hard days, and to keep pushing forwards. It still motivates me to this day and I maintain a healthy obsession with self-help books! I love soaking up lessons on how other successful people operate, how they spend their time, and how they stay motivated. Even if I glean just one helpful nugget from a book, I consider it a good use of my time.

I also credit my life coach with being a major source of inspiration and motivation. If you have the means to work with a life coach, I highly recommend it. If you're in the UK, the Life Coach Directory (www.lifecoach-directory.org.uk) is a useful resource.

Much as I love my life coach, I also know that having an in-person mentor would have helped me grow my business more rapidly in the early days. So I encourage you to find a mentor of your own - whether that's a paid-for mentorship programme, or a less formal mentorship relationship.

Your mentor doesn't have to be an entrepreneur or a career-focused mentor - not if that doesn't tie in with your goals. The right mentor for you is anyone who motivates you to be the best you can be. Anyone you can learn from as you climb up from rock bottom. It could be that friend who's deep into meditation and yoga. It could be someone you know who successfully juggles a busy life while making time for their self-care. It could be someone who's incredibly creative.

Identify the person or people who could act in an inspiring mentorship role – either as a formal mentor, or just someone you meet for coffee once a month and pick their brains. It's all good.

While I didn't have a mentor when I was starting out, I have found people to meet that mentorship need over the years. For example, I've partnered with investors who are operating on a bigger scale than me and have learned so much in the process. And in another example, I mentioned that I create educational content for YouTube and my own property courses; well, in time, that led to me presenting a TV programme with *Homes Under the Hammer* presenter Martin Roberts. Martin has been on national daytime TV in the UK for over 20 years and working with him is both educational and inspiring. I see him as a sort of 'media mentor', helping me to hone my presentation skills and become more comfortable in front of the camera.

I have to acknowledge that there may be a cost associated with some of these relationships. You'd have to pay for a life coach, for example, or to secure a place on certain mentorship programmes (including my own). My advice is to not shy away from paid-for opportunities like this if you believe they will be valuable for you. In fact, investing financially in your journey can create a snowball effect – as in, by actively building relationships with inspiring people, you attract more inspiring people your way.

CONNECTING WITH PRACTICAL SUPPORT

Depending on your goals, you may also need practical, expert support to guide you and keep you on the right track. Like Bill hiring a virtual PA because he knew that trying to do everything himself would only sap his motivation. Similarly, Bill was connecting with people who were experts in bushcraft and other outdoor skills, because those were the people who could help him grow his charity.

The equivalent for you could be hiring a personal trainer to help you stay committed to your fitness journey. Or connecting with a videographer who can help you create professional content. Or hiring a freelance marketer, book editor, writing coach, or whomever.

These are people who can help you elevate your own skills and stay committed to your journey. And sometimes, they're the people who can take certain things off your plate so you can focus on the things that really matter.

Especially if your goal is to become a successful entrepreneur, I urge you to get good at delegating and outsourcing tasks. Work out which areas are the best use of your time or which areas you particularly want to focus on (because you love doing those things or they're very important to you) - and then outsource the rest. Or as much of the rest as possible.

Over the years I've built a team of freelancers and experts around me who help me do what I do. They keep me honest. They ensure I do the things I say I'm going to do. And they allow me to focus my time and energy where I can have the most impact - and that, perhaps above all else, helps me stay motivated. I'm not bogged down in the nitty gritty tasks that I don't particularly enjoy - things like vetting tenants or chasing up suppliers or doing my tax return. I let the experts take care of those tasks so I can focus on what I do best - which is growing my business, growing my personal brand, and (dare I say) writing books like this. I call this growing band of practical support stars my Dream Team or my Power Team. And I consider them to be a hugely valuable part of my business.

Yes, there's a cost associated with outsourcing tasks but - and forgive me for shouting it out here - YOUR TIME IS VALUABLE TOO. If you never have time for the things that matter to you because you're too busy doing other things, you will struggle to stay motivated and committed to your journey. So how can you shift things off your plate to make space for the things that matter? Could you, for example, hire someone to clean your house, freeing up two hours a week where you can focus on your continual learning? Or could you do a babysitting swap with a friend, giving you a whole evening a week to focus on your goals or self-care?

Allow yourself to lean on others for practical support, whether that's support that you pay for, or calling in favours when you need them. Allow yourself that. Ask for help. And watch as people rally around you.

OTHER WAYS TO MAINTAIN MOMENTUM

Okay, I think by now I've emphasised the message that you will absolutely need other people to help you on your journey. You're far more likely to stay committed and motivated if you bring other people along with you.

But here are some other tips to help you stay motivated.

- Create and maintain a routine that supports your goals (refer back to Chapter 7 for this).
- Try not to get overwhelmed by the bigger picture or the end destination. Take your journey one step at a time and have faith that, if you put in the work, you *will* achieve everything you desire (revisit Chapters 9 and 10 for a refresher on this).
- Use visualisation and the dream board as a way to build excitement about your goals. I find that creating a clear mental picture of the things I want does wonders for my motivation (again, see Chapter 10).
- Check in with your goals – and your why – on a regular basis. Perhaps the reason you're struggling with a particular goal is because it doesn't really connect with your why (see Chapter 5).
- Continue to set new goals that challenge and inspire you. These don't have to be big, life-changing goals – just something that keeps things interesting. For example, if you've started jogging, you could

- sign up for one of those charity fun runs where everyone throws paint at each other!
- Remind yourself of how far you've come. I love looking ahead, but sometimes looking back at how far I've travelled delivers a massive shot of motivation. Look at how far you've already travelled on your journey from rock bottom. And if you're still in the very early days, hey, you picked up this book and made a commitment to building an awesome life. That's no small thing. Be proud.
- Surround yourself with positive people. I'm not only talking about people who inspire you, or give you practical or emotional support – but also people who are positive and have a can-do attitude. If you have an optimistic Aunt Mable who always looks on the bright side of life, maybe you should spend a bit more time around her rather than Negative Cousin Ned.
- Set time limits on your social media. Listen, I love social media and use it all the time for my business. In fact, it's been a core part of growing my brand. But I can't deny that social media is a time suck. And it can, at times, make me feel anxious about the state of the world, or wonder if the grass might be greener in someone else's garden. None of which is good for motivation. I'm not saying you have to come off social media altogether, but set yourself time limits – most smart phones have a setting where you can set time limits for specific apps.
- Reframe failure. Just a reminder here that not everything will go your way on the climb from rock bottom, but that's okay – failure does not define you. So when you do hit a bump in the road, don't let that demotivate you. Because if you never really fail, you're never really pushing yourself. By all means learn from mistakes and failures, but then dust yourself off and keep on moving.

THE PROCRASTINATION TRAP

Another side of staying motivated is overcoming procrastination. In other words, the biggest obstacle to your motivation could be ... you. Your desire to stay safe in the status quo, stay safe in your comfort zone, and avoid change. To put things off for another day, another week. Pretty soon, your motivation and good intentions slip away.

There's an old saying that 'Procrastination is the thief of time.' I prefer to think of procrastination as the thief of dreams.

The best way to fight procrastination and stick to your goals is to make your comfortable status quo, well, *uncomfortable*. Make it so that you *have* to move forwards out of your comfort zone.

I find understanding push and pull motivators is helpful in the battle against procrastination (see Chapter 8 for more on push and pull motivators). To be pushed out of procrastination, you need something that makes your comfort zone uncomfortable. This could be the risk of not paying your rent on time, or missing an important deadline, or something similar. Alternatively, to be pulled out of procrastination, you need something that's more desirable than your comfort zone, something pulling you forward - which is where your dream board and visualisation exercises can help.

You may be motivated more by push motivators than pull motivators, or vice versa. And that's fine. Just a reminder to use this to your advantage in the fight against procrastination.

The above tips for staying motivated will also help you overcome procrastination. But perhaps the biggest thing you can do is recognise procrastination when it occurs. Whenever that little voice in your head tells you something can wait, or it's not that important (when you know deep down that it is), recognise that voice for what it really is - the thief of your dreams.

LESSONS FROM THE CLIMB

- Going it alone when you hit rock bottom is rarely the best strategy. You need people who will lift you up, help you stay motivated, and

keep you on track. You need to build a support team around you. Because people are the secret weapon when it comes to staying motivated.
- Don't be afraid of sharing your struggles or weaknesses with others. The more you open yourself up to others, the more love and support will flow your way.
- Your personal support network may include: people who inspire you (for example, a mentor, life coach or other inspirational figures who you may not even know in real life); people who give you emotional support (such as a therapist, support group or loved ones); and people who can give you practical support when you need it (which may include childcare, a personal trainer, freelance support services, and a whole lot more).
- Other ways to stay motivated include sticking to a routine; staying connected to your goals and your why; using visualisation and other mindset tools; reminding yourself of how far you've come; limiting social media time; and reframing failure.
- You may also need strategies to help you overcome procrastination. Most importantly, recognise procrastination when it occurs - and remember, procrastination is the thief of your dreams.

As I've alluded to in this chapter, another important facet of the climb from rock bottom is helping others up along the way. So let's explore this topic in more detail and see why it's so important to lift others up, even when you experience your own struggles…

Chapter 12

HELPING OTHERS ALONG THE WAY

Bill's daughter Callie, now a thriving 14-year-old, carried the tent-shaped cake towards Bill as everyone in the room cheered and clapped.

But this wasn't a birthday party. This was a gathering of friends and employees to celebrate the opening of this new space – official premises for Bill's charity. By this point, the charity employed a counsellor, an event coordinator, a fundraiser and an admin assistant. And Bill, of course. Because he was no longer working in his corporate job. He was now full-time CEO of the charity he'd started.

This was a big milestone for Bill and his team. After months of working from their separate homes, gathering around Bill's kitchen table, and pitching up in coworking spaces, they now had an office of their own. A place close to the high street where people could enquire about upcoming nature events, sign up as a volunteer, buy merchandise (all part of fundraising), or just simply have a coffee and chat. It was a cool, modern, open-plan space – part-office, part-coffee shop, part-community hub. Bill was really proud.

And the charity was doing so well that Bill had expanded the scope to include young people. He was now working with several local schools to run nature and mindfulness excursions.

Bill had plans even bigger than that. He was eyeing expansion beyond the local town. Eventually, to a national scale.

REACHING BACK DOWN TO HELP OTHERS

Bill blushed as he took the cake and thanked his daughter. She'd made it herself.

'Speech!' cried someone in the room.

'Um...' Bill said.

The single cry turned into a chorus: 'Speech, speech!'

'Well...' Bill paused. 'A little over two years ago, my world turned upside down. If you'd told me then that this is where I'd be, I'd have thought you were crazy. I never pictured myself running a non-profit. To be honest, I never really gave much of my time or money to charity. My working life was the very opposite of this. And my non-work life was pretty insular, as it so often is when life is busy and fast-paced.'

There were nods of recognition from the audience.

Bill continued, 'My focus really went inwards when I hit rock bottom. You spend a lot of time thinking about yourself when you hit the bottom - trying to figure out what to do and where to go next. The climb back takes a lot of introspection. Learning to love yourself, take care of your needs, and figure out the kind of life you want to build - you have to go deep inside and really understand yourself. You get a bit selfish, even. You're working on yourself and it feels good to pay yourself that attention.'

He paused. 'The danger is you can get so intensely wrapped up in your journey that you might forget to consider others. Yet, on the climb from rock bottom is exactly when you should be helping others, being kind, being compassionate, reaching back down to bring others up with you. Because ... well, it's really bloody good for you!'

The crowd laughed.

'Seriously,' Bill continued. 'I'm so grateful that I found this purpose relatively early in my journey. That I've been able to help others as I've helped myself up out of rock bottom. It's benefitted those people, I know. But it's benefitted me even more. I've gained more than I've given. And I can't wait to keep going, thank you.'

The crowd applauded.

'Alright, let's cut this gorgeous cake,' Bill said.

DON'T WAIT UNTIL YOU REACH THE TOP

'Great speech,' I said later. 'Give back to get more. Very inspiring.'

'Thanks,' Bill smiled. 'Do you like it?' He meant the office.

I nodded enthusiastically. 'It's perfect. You've done an amazing job.'

'Well, my team, mostly,' Bill replied. 'And Callie, she tiled that coffee counter over there.'

'Really?' I asked.

'Yeah, she watched a YouTube video on how to do it and away she went.' He laughed and shook his head. 'Kids are amazing.'

'It's great that she's involved here.'

Bill agreed. 'I really want her to learn this lesson early in life - earlier than I did - that you don't have to be successful or rich to give back to others. I find it crazy that people think you can only help people once you've achieved everything you want. Like how people say they'll support a charity when they win the lottery, or donate their time when they no longer work full-time. I think they're missing the point.'

'Which is?' I prompted.

'That no matter how low you are, no matter how bad things seem, there is always someone out there whom you could help in one way or another. Doesn't have to be giving money or donating time. It could be taking the recycling bins in for an elderly neighbour, or cooking a meal for a friend with a newborn baby. Anything. Just help where you can. And don't put it off until you have the time, or money, or freedom. Do it on your way up. Bring others up alongside you.'

'Don't wait until you reach the top,' I said.

'Exactly!' Bill said. 'Even just smiling at people more. Saying good morning. I try to do more and more of these little giving moments. That's what I call them, "giving moments". And I feel great as a result. I mean, I'm not saying you should only give back for selfish reasons, but I can't deny it makes me feel good. And the more of these little moments that I put out there – you know, smiling at people, offering to help with a heavy bag, or whatever – I notice more kindnesses in return. And it spurs me on to do even better.'

GIVING BACK BRINGS MORE GOOD STUFF YOUR WAY

'It's very law of attraction,' I said. 'The more good stuff you put out there, the more good stuff is returned to you. It makes sense from a business point of view as well.'

'How do you mean?' Bill asked.

'You know, the most successful and best-known companies in the world are those that solve problems and make life better for as many people as possible – whether it's Google offering free email to the masses, or Apple making phones that are so advanced, they're basically portable computers. They're not doing it for philanthropic reasons, I get that, but by offering very real benefits to people, they reap so many rewards in return.'

'Interesting,' Bill said. 'I never thought of it that way.'

'But that's what you're doing here, basically. You set out to help small groups of men at a time, but have since grown that to include local young people. You're looking even wider than that, beyond the local area. And good for you - because the more people you help, the more successful and rewarded you'll be in return.'

'The law of attraction,' Bill said.

'Precisely,' I agreed. 'But it's not just good from a law of attraction perspective. Like you said, giving feels good.'

Bill laughed. 'Oh my, I've gone down such a rabbit hole on the topic of giving. I'm fascinated by it. Did you know that giving provokes a neurological response?'

'I did not,' I said.

'There have been all these studies done on the benefits of giving, and they've shown that there's a link between giving and the release of neurochemical drivers of happiness. Happy hormones, basically. So when I help someone or show someone kindness, my brain releases dopamine, serotonin and oxytocin - and these result in a mood boost. It's called "helper's high". Helping and giving increases self-esteem, boosts happiness, and combats depression. Which is why I'm so passionate that people should help others on the way up. Which is also why I encourage my clients to find their own giving moments. In fact, some are going to be volunteering here.'

'Amazing,' I said. 'I'm really proud of what you've created here. There's huge value in this.'

'Well, that's another benefit, isn't it?' Bill said. 'The realisation that I am useful, that I do have something to offer. That feeling has been really helpful these last two years. There were so many times when I felt worthless or useless, just lost at sea. Not even sure of who I was. Doing all this and finding lots of little giving moments allows me to feel pride and happiness as often as possible. It's the best thing I've found for banishing negative feelings.'

HELPING OTHERS ON YOUR CLIMB

Being at rock bottom nearly always provokes a change. A change of circumstances, finances, mental state, physical health, relationship status, career, or whatever. Change doesn't always feel like a good thing, especially when it's thrust on you, but the good news is change opens up space - space for you to create who you want to be. And as part of creating this new you, and the life you desire, I urge you to become someone who gives, helps and serves others.

This doesn't mean you have to completely uproot your career and start a charity, as Bill did. It doesn't necessarily mean donating money to charity every month. Or volunteering several evenings a week at the local homeless shelter. You can give in lots of small ways. Give support. Give encouragement. Give a smile. Give a helping hand. Give someone the phone number of your amazing plumber. Give a colleague a leg up. Give away the possessions you no longer need.

And if you can give money, great. It may seem counterintuitive, but giving money away can bring *more* prosperity to you, not less. By giving money - however little - you're saying 'I have enough'. And that's a powerful sentiment to put out into the universe. As the law of attraction teaches us, if you say you're too poor to give money, you will likely attract more of the same: poverty, money stresses. But by saying 'I have plenty', 'I'm doing well', 'I have what I need as I work towards the things I want' you attract abundance.

Because those who give to others get more back in return. Helping others brings more good things your way.

Whatever and however you help others, the key thing is to start now, at this point on your journey. Don't wait until you're successful. Don't wait until you've reached the summit of your climb. Help others climb up with you. Aside from attracting good things to you, it's a great way to combat depression and negative feelings. This is scientifically proven.

And it can give you those feelings of being proud, being needed, being of value to people - if those are feelings that you currently lack. Tap into that 'helper's high' and enjoy the buzz.

YOU GET BACK WHAT YOU PUT OUT THERE

Let's briefly return to the law of attraction (Chapter 10) and the idea that you get back what you put out there.

What are you putting out there most days? You're putting out thoughts, words and actions all the time. But what else? Are you putting your time, energy and attention out there? Are you, for example, giving back to your industry by mentoring up-and-coming colleagues? Are you giving back to your community by donating food to the local food bank? Are you giving back to your partner by saying, 'How can I make today better for you?' Are you giving back to your friends by saying, 'I appreciate you'?

Or is your time, energy and attention focused mostly inwards? Looking inwards and understanding your needs is certainly a positive move when you hit rock bottom - especially in the early days. But as you begin to pull away from rock bottom and step towards your future, your focus shouldn't be entirely inwards, on yourself. Not at all.

My point is, look at where you send your time, energy and attention, so that you can strike a balance between serving your needs, and serving others.

Show up for others and they'll show up for you. Like attracts like.

Because by saying things like 'I'm too busy to help' you're only attracting more time pressures your way. By saying 'I'm too tired to call my friend. I'll call them next week,' you're attracting more tiredness (and poorer relationships).

By the way, I'm not implying that you can never say 'no' to people. If there's a situation where you genuinely can't do something, it's perfectly okay to have boundaries. Giving back isn't about running yourself into the ground. Again, it's about balance - and understanding that how you direct your time, energy and attention matters. That's what the law of attraction teaches us.

In a similar way, when you're doing well in life, hoarding that success for yourself - worrying that others might take a piece of your hard-earned pie - is counterintuitive. Because if you worry about losing what you have, that's probably what will happen. Which is why, as part of my business, I deliberately give away lots of property advice for free or publish affordable books like this. I'm not trying to keep the secrets of success to myself and keep other people down. That's not the way to attract more success to me.

There's plenty of success to go around for everyone. I firmly believe that. And by adopting that attitude - by shaping my business around it - I attract more success and abundance to myself.

As motivational speaker Brian Tracy put it, 'Successful people are always looking for opportunities to help others. Unsuccessful people are always asking "what's in it for me?"'

That's partly how the Extraordinary Millionaire project came about (www.extraordinarymillionaire.com). When my business partners and I first started imagining The Extraordinary Millionaire, one thought was always top of our minds: how can we help others? Based on our experience, we felt that one of the most impactful ways we could serve people was through financial education and mindset advice. For us, it's a way to give back and say thank you for the lives we have.

In fact, that's a critical point: giving back to others is an *act of gratitude*. I'm saying thank you for everything I have in my life that allows me to give to others - whether it's giving part of the profits from this book to charity, giving my time and driving half-way across Europe to deliver supplies to Ukrainian refuges in Poland (truly a memorable and moving experience), or giving away success-building advice. In those acts, I'm expressing my gratitude for the life I have. I'm living with a mindset of plenty. And in the process, I bring even more my way.

Remember the final step in the law of attraction process: ask, believe, receive? Receive means to live your life as though you already have everything you desire. Live that life now as you work to manifest your dreams. Feel good. Feel content. Feel positive. Giving back and helping others on your climb is a great way to put that step into practice.

ADDING VALUE AS A WAY TO GIVE BACK

There's another hugely impactful way to give back - and that is to add value through what you do. Whatever your job, how can you better serve others through that work? How can you apply that ethos to serve more people or solve more problems?

I believe you can think like this and seek to add value in any job. But it's especially applicable if you want to become an entrepreneur. If you have ambitions of starting a business, my advice to you is this: find a way to help as many people as possible with your product or service. And, again, that doesn't mean philanthropically (although it might) - it can simply mean adding value to people's lives or making their lives easier in some way.

That's what Google does with its search engine and email service. It's free, it's highly effective and its easily accessible. Sure, Google profits in return for providing this thoughtful service. Why shouldn't Google profit in return? But they clearly set out to build a product that would be valuable to as many people as possible. And it worked.

So, if you can, find a way to align your goals with this idea of adding value. Ask yourself how you can offer as much value as possible to as many people as possible. It's good business sense. It makes sense from a law of attraction perspective. And, I'll be honest, it feels great to add value for others.

Sounds totally obvious, doesn't it? You should do a good job and provide a valuable product or service to customers. And yet I see so many shoddy operators who are just out to make a fast buck and really don't care whether they deliver value or not.

If you think about it, it's actually quite a common sentiment that crops up in business - that the secret to success is to only look out for number one. Screw other people!

Which is probably why I see so many 'experts' offering courses that promise to unlock the secrets of wealth and make people wildly rich overnight. Courses that cost thousands of pounds. Yet, in reality, some of those courses take self-help books, regurgitate the headline points as a slideshow, and then slap a four-figure price tag on it. Where's the value in that, when the customer could buy a book for £15 and get the same information? And at the end of it all, they won't get rich overnight. Because no one ever does. Growing your wealth and becoming financially independent takes time and effort.

I strongly disagree with that sort of unethical approach - over-promising and under-delivering. Through the Wealth Labs platform, through my courses, through my free content, and through paid-for content like this, I want to provide genuine value for people. Within that there are opportunities to grow my own financial and career success. I don't think there's anything wrong with that. If you like this book, for instance, you might recommend it to a friend who then buys it. That's another book sale for me. Then based on how much they like the book, that friend might go on to pay for one of my courses. By adding value for readers, I gain a wider audience, grow my brand, build more trust in my products, and ultimately grow the success of my business. It's win-win. (By the way, I talk more about this in my book, *The Extraordinary Millionaire*.)

Bottom line, adding value is a fantastic way to give back to others and is something you can weave into business and career success, if that forms part of your goals.

Giving money to charity, buying a coffee for a homeless guy, helping a friend in need ... those are all great ways to achieve that 'helper's high' and attract more positivity into your life. But if one of your goals is to become hugely successful, I urge you to also think about this concept of adding as much value as possible, through your product or service, for as many people as possible. That way lies major success.

LESSONS FROM THE CLIMB

- It's vital you reach down and help others on your climb from rock bottom. Giving back and helping others produces massive mental health benefits – and from a law of attraction perspective, it brings more good things your way.
- Don't wait until you become successful before you help others. Don't wait until you reach the top. Start now. Help others as you help yourself up from rock bottom.
- Giving back can mean giving time and money. Or it can mean giving your attention and energy to someone who needs help. Giving someone a smile and serving them in a small way. It can mean giving appreciation to others.
- Giving back is an act of gratitude. It is saying thank you for the things you have in your life that allow you to give back. As such, it's a great way to put the law of attraction into practice. By giving back, and living as though you have an abundant life – abundant in time, energy, love, money, whatever – you attract more abundance to you.
- Another way to give back is to add value through what you do. If you want to become super-successful in your career, you need to find a way to help as many people as possible and add as much value as possible. Success doesn't come from pushing others down or trying to get one over on people for profit; success comes from lifting others up.

We're almost at the end of Bill's story, but there's one more lesson to cover. One major life lesson that shaped Bill's ongoing journey – and should shape yours too. Turn the page to discover what it is…

Part IV
The Journey

TAKING PLEASURE IN THE PROCESS, NOT JUST THE RESULTS

'Life is a journey, not a destination. Happiness is not "there" but here, not "tomorrow" but today.'

–SIDNEY GREENBERG

Chapter 13

WHY LIVING IS THE JOURNEY

I was dropping my daughter off at Bill's house for Callie's end-of-GCSEs party.

'Why don't you come in for a drink?' Bill asked. 'There are a few adults here cramping the teenagers' style.'

My daughter shot me a warning look. One of those *go away, Dad* looks.

'Love to,' I said. 'Just a quick one.'

My daughter rolled her eyes and went off to find Callie.

It was all go in the garden. There was music playing, balloons and festoon lights strung above the lawn, teenagers everywhere. Bill had even hired a flower archway for the Instagram-conscious teens to take selfies.

Meanwhile, the adults clustered in the kitchen. There were some family members and friends, a couple of other parents who had lingered to check out what was going on, and over at the kitchen table, mixing up a suspicious-looking punch, was Bill's ex-wife Tina and her partner Greg. Bill reached past Tina for a beer and they exchanged a few words. I couldn't hear what they said, but they were smiling. Bill said something and she laughed her explosive laugh in response, then they both looked out to the garden at Callie and her friends. Greg offered to open the bottle of beer and Bill passed it to him with a smile. They looked relaxed in each other's company. A modern, complicated family.

'Thanks,' I said, as Bill brought the beer over to me. 'Nice to see you co-hosting this thing together.'

'It's all gone pretty smoothly actually,' Bill said. 'I think we only had one argument, and that was over how much alcohol was allowed. Otherwise, it's been good. It's nice for Callie that we can do it this way. And besides, it helps to split the cost. Wait, why are you smiling at me like that?'

'Because this is the sort of thing you were visualising years ago,' I said. 'Having a cordial relationship with your ex-wife. Being proud together of the person you raised. You're here. You've arrived at your destination. Enjoy this moment.'

'You're right,' Bill said. 'It's a nice moment to enjoy. You're wrong about the other thing, though.'

'And what's that?' I asked.

LIVING IN THE HERE AND NOW

'This isn't my destination,' Bill clarified. 'I don't know if I'll ever reach one big "destination" as such. There'll be milestones, of course. This is one of them. But as I achieve one milestone or goal, there will be others. It's all just one big journey, isn't it?'

'I suppose it is,' I replied.

'Which is why we need to enjoy the journey itself. I think that's the most eye-opening lesson I've learned these past few years. The one lesson that transformed hitting rock bottom into the best thing that ever happened to me: living is in the journey, not the destination. I won't be "living" once I reach all my goals. I'm living right now. In this step of my journey, and the next step, and so on. Life *is* the journey.'

'In which case,' I said, 'we all need to find joy in the here and now, not just focus on where we're heading.'

'Exactly,' Bill said. 'It's not always easy to be present in the here and now. Especially as the charity takes off and I begin to set more ambitious goals. But I'm taking care to remind myself every day that, while those future goals matter a great deal, life happens in the journey. Life isn't in some future destination. There is no *one* destination. Life is here, now. I need to appreciate it.'

He continued, 'I look back at my life before and I see someone who constantly overlooked the little things in life because they seemed so small and insignificant in the bigger scheme of things. I'd pass on opportunities to try new things because I was too busy. I'd be so wrapped up in meeting certain career goals or targets, so focused on the results, I didn't take the chance to enjoy the journey.'

'God, that reminds me of someone else I know,' I said. 'You don't know him, but he and his wife joined us on our holiday last week.'

'Oh yeah?' Bill asked.

I explained, 'So the weather in Holland was terrible. It was muddy everywhere. We were staying in these old-school chalet things. It was hardly a dream holiday scenario. So the best approach was to just throw ourselves into it. Get muddy. Get wet. Get tipsy. Enjoy the food. Enjoy the time together.'

'But your friend couldn't?'

'He was always in the next moment, or the next day. He'd constantly say things like "I'm putting on too much weight on this holiday" "I'm going on a diet next week" "Tomorrow I'm going to drink less" "I'll have to burn all this off in the morning." I get it, he's a health-conscious guy and it was pissing down most of the time so we all indulged a little more than normal. But he was never happy in the moment. It was kind of a buzzkill.'

'I can imagine,' Bill said. 'Actually, the body and dieting is a pretty good analogy for this whole thing. You may be working towards a better, healthier, stronger body, and that's great. But you can still love and appreciate the body you're in right now.'

OVERCOMING OUR PROGRAMMING

'I love that,' I said. 'I think the reason so many people struggle with that concept is we're taught from a young age to always be looking ahead.'

'True,' Bill agreed.

'I mean, when we're young we're taught to look ahead to different milestones. "You can't do X, Y and Z until you're 16", that sort of thing. We constantly ask children what they want to be when they grow up - and I'm as guilty of this as the next person - but all it does is reinforce this idea that adulthood is a destination. When they should be enjoying being a child.'

Bill thought for a moment. 'Maybe we should be asking them what they want to be *now* instead?'

I nodded. 'And then at school we get taught how to pass our exams so we can move on to the next year or the next grade. All the while we're encouraged to think about university and life after school. We're constantly taught to think about the next stage of life, to move on, to get this part of the journey over with. No wonder this carries over into adulthood. Finish school, go to uni, get a good job, get married, buy a house, have kids. Always thinking about the next stage. And meanwhile, life passes us by.'

'Until,' Bill said, 'you hit rock bottom and things come crashing down around your ears. The next phase of life, one that previously seemed so certain, suddenly disappears. That's why I think of rock bottom as the best thing that happened to me. I could have got back on the horse and rebuilt my life in the same way - always concentrating on the destination. But instead I was able to stop, recalibrate and come out the other side as someone who's able to appreciate the journey.'

'Enjoying the process, not just the results,' I said. 'I'll drink to that.'

'Cheers!'

WHAT BILL DID NEXT

This is where we leave Bill, standing in his kitchen, watching his daughter pose for selfies with her friends, as the sounds of teenage laughter and terrible music wafted into the house.

Bill didn't know at this point that his charity would go on to achieve new heights, and ultimately become a leading national charity empowering people to heal through nature. Bill didn't know that he would build a name for himself in this area, being invited onto radio shows and podcasts to talk about the importance of nature, mindfulness and making time for yourself in a busy world. Five years from now, Bill would be invited to write a book on the topic. A year after that he would marry Claudia, an accountant-turned-yoga teacher who had been on her own journey of self-discovery.

Together, they would dream up exciting new possibilities for the future, without losing sight of the present.

ENJOYING YOUR JOURNEY

We've talked so much about goals in this book. I'm someone who loves to set goals and challenge myself. I love looking ahead to the future and visualising specific goals coming to life. It drives me on. It makes me feel more positive. I enjoy having things to look forward to.

But it's also important to me that I can be present in the here and now. Like my friend Bill - and *unlike* my friend from my chalet holiday - I want to enjoy the little moments, enjoy the process, enjoy the journey as I travel it. Because my happiness doesn't lie in some future event or achievement. It's here, today.

So my final piece of advice for you is this: enjoy your journey as best you can. Don't treat your climb from rock bottom - or any phase of your life - as something to 'get done' as quickly as possible. This isn't a punishment or boot camp. This is your life. Enjoy it now. Even as you work to build the life of your dreams, enjoy it as it is now. Find those micro-moments of peace and satisfaction wherever you can. Notice more. Notice as much as you can. Appreciate more.

I realise this can seem like obvious advice. And yet how many of us go through life on autopilot in the present, focusing our attention instead on some future event, milestone or goal?

And listen, I understand that it's easier to enjoy a journey when that journey is of your choosing. If you're studying for your dream career, it's a hell of a lot easier to enjoy that journey than if you've been thrust into the job market after being made redundant. The journeys we choose are easier to embrace. I've had a taste of this myself lately.

OBSTACLES BRING OPPORTUNITIES

My wife and I recently sold our dream family home - a home that we absolutely loved and stretched ourselves to buy. Much as we loved the home, we were moving our family to Holland, to be closer to my wife's family, so the time had come to sell up. We accepted an offer on the basis that we would exchange contracts within one month and complete the sale within two months. Instead, it took us six months to get to the point of exchanging contracts. And in the meantime, we were unable to plan this big life change. We didn't know if the sale would go through, and therefore, what our financial situation would be. We didn't know what school the kids would be at in six months' time - if they'd be staying in their local schools or starting school in Holland.

Getting through those months was tough. A long, drawn-out process like that certainly wasn't of my choosing - and it's journeys like that which I personally find the hardest.

Were there times when I'd wish the week or month away so we could move one step closer to our exciting family move? Of course there were, I'm not perfect! But even as we muscled through the discomfort and the uncertainty, I still worked at finding moments of satisfaction and comfort. I tried to see each delaying phone call from the estate agent as an opportunity to control my emotions and choose my mindset. Because I know that if I can do that, I can do anything.

And I look back now – having moved my family to Holland and with us about to get the keys to our new family home – and feel proud that we got through it as a family, without losing our sanity (too often).

There have been obstacles in my working life, too, that created a lot of discomfort and uncertainty in the present. In one example, we finished a development project and started filling it with tenants, but then the local council challenged us saying our use of the property wasn't lawful – when we knew it was. My team and I had to get a barrister's opinion and fight the council to prove that we were well within the law. For several months we were at risk of losing the development, and in the meantime, we weren't able to put tenants in there. Which meant no income. A delay like that can cause serious cash flow issues for a developer like me – we were on the brink of cash flow bankruptcy. (By cash flow bankruptcy I mean we still had plenty of assets in our portfolio, but our cash flow was becoming increasingly precarious.)

In the end we successfully fought the council. Our development was declared legal. And we ended up selling the building for a profit of over a million pounds. But imagine the emotions of that journey, from a precarious financial position to a million-pound profit. It was a rollercoaster, and it would have been all too easy to wish those months away, to get it over with as quickly as possible. To focus only on the future.

Having faith in the end goal kept me going in the present, but so too did finding joy in the little moments. Like a cuddle with my kids. Or going fishing. I tried hard to be present in the journey, even though it wasn't a journey of my choosing.

It helped to understand that the obstacle facing me was actually an opportunity to learn. Thanks to this project, I now know how to fight a council. I now know how to work with a barrister. I'm a better developer as a result of this project, and that will feed into my mentorship work and courses. I can see that this incredibly stressful project has brought me huge benefits (aside from the profit), and I'm grateful for that.

SO HOW CAN YOU ENJOY THE JOURNEY, EVEN WHEN IT'S HARD?

Many of the tools in this book will help you find contentment or even joy in the small moments. Build a practice of gratitude and mindfulness, for instance, and that will serve you well on your journey, in good times and bad. Visualisation will help you keep faith in your goals and feel more positive - which in turn, makes it easier to enjoy the here and now, because you know you will, in time, manifest the things you want. As the law of attraction says, relax into the certainty that the universe will deliver and feel good now.

You also need to get comfortable with the fact that you are on a journey. Remind yourself of that regularly. Remind yourself that life is in the journey. It's today, not tomorrow or in five years' time when you're free of debt/thinner and fitter/a successful entrepreneur or whatever. Yes, you will feel enormous satisfaction when you achieve your goals. But you can tap into that satisfaction now, too.

In addition, I find it helps to work on being self-aware. Check in with your thoughts and feelings on a regular basis. Are you acting from a place of anxiety, for example? (Which is a good sign that your attention is perhaps focused too hard on the future.) Or are you feeling pretty relaxed right now? In which case, notice and enjoy that feeling. How nice it is to feel your shoulders loosen and your mind be still for a moment.

Another tip is to be at ease with who you are *right now*, in this moment. That holiday with my health-conscious friend? Yes, I came back from that holiday with my trousers feeling a little tighter than I'd like. (It didn't help that my family had been living in temporary accommodation for months before that, without our usual kitchen setup. Healthy eating had fallen by the wayside for more than just that week's holiday.) But I wasn't going to let it ruin my post-holiday mood. I know when we settle into our new home, and have a full working kitchen again, we'll ease back into our usual family routine of eating nourishing homecooked food more often than not. My trousers will soon be comfortable again! Importantly, I'll enjoy that process of getting back into healthy eating and dropping a few pounds. I won't be a grumpy dieter, feeling deprived and punished and hungry. I'll be thankful for the opportunity and means to cook good food and I'll be proud of every achievement as I go. Even more importantly, in the meantime, I'm happy with who I am *now*.

(A caveat here that, of course, many people struggle with their mental health and self-image. Overcoming depression, for example, isn't just a case of me telling you to be happy in the here and now. So do recognise when you need professional help, and seek that help.)

And my final tip is to remember to take action towards your goals. Enjoy the journey, but make sure you're progressing along your path.

ONWARDS WITH YOUR JOURNEY

I really feel like we've been on a journey together, you, Bill and I. Hopefully you feel the same. But since we're about to say goodbye, part ways, and continue on our individual paths, I wanted to leave you with some parting words of inspiration.

Take a deep breath in this moment. Breathe deeply and recognise that the climb up from rock bottom ... that's what life is. You'll hit exciting highs. You'll probably slip back down here and there. It's all part of the journey, part of life. Your satisfaction doesn't lie at the top of the mountain, it's with you on the climb.

Every new high and every slip back down is a new opportunity to learn and grow. You may even hit rock bottom again. If that happens, it's okay. You have your blueprint - this book - to help you climb back up again. Do the work and there will absolutely be new beginnings, new relationships, new opportunities, and new growth.

Rock bottom is your chance not to rebuild, but to *reimagine*. Or to put it another way, rock bottom hasn't happened to you, it's happened *for* you.

Life has given you a shove for a reason, so take this time to learn the lesson that life is trying to teach you. Instead of rebuilding more of the same - another job, another marriage, etc. - reimagine a lifestyle that fills every bit of your being with purpose and passion. Create the you that you've always wanted to be. You're in control. No one else can do this journey for you. And no one can stop you but you.

So create that future vision that fills you with excitement. But don't chase the destination at the expense of the journey. Because the journey is where life happens.

LESSONS FOR THE REST OF YOUR LIFE

- Rock bottom didn't happen to you, it happened *for* you. This is your opportunity to create change and build the life you want.
- But remember that life is not the destination, it's the journey. Your happiness and fulfilment do not lie in some future milestone or achievement. It's here, now.
- Don't treat your climb from rock bottom - or any phase of your life - as something to 'get done' as quickly as possible. There is joy in the process.
- Find ways to be present in the here and now. To enjoy the little moments as you work towards the bigger milestones. Mindfulness and gratitude are great for this. Plus, visualisation and the law of attraction will help you cultivate that feeling of certainty that you *will* achieve the life you desire - which helps you relax into the current moment.
- Be comfortable in who you are now. Yes, you're on a journey of self-improvement, and that's amazing, but also learn to love and accept the current you.

What To Read Next

We'd love to take this opportunity to recommend another book in this series: *The Extraordinary Millionaire: Harness the REAL tools for success, grow your wealth and build an extraordinary life.* It's written for people who want to escape the rat race, become financially independent and generally build a more fulfilling life. You'll recognise some of the mindset tools from this book, but it also delves into wealth creation and business success, if that appeals to you.

Head to www.extraordinarymillionaire.com to find out more about the Extraordinary Millionaire series.

Connect With Us

If you have questions or find yourself unsure of how to implement some of the steps into your daily routine, please reach out to us.

We would also love to hear what you think about the book. Which chapters resonated with you? Which bits made you sit up and say 'Yes! I've been there!' Which parts made the most difference on your own journey from rock bottom?

You can connect with Nicholas on Instagram (@nicholas_wallwork), on LinkedIn or via nicholaswallwork.com

You can connect with Martin via www.linkedin.com/in/martinfosterwealth or through our website www.extraordinarymillioniare.com (incidentally, this is also where you can find details about the other books, classes, coaching and mentorship programmes in the Extraordinary Millionaire Series).

We can't wait to hear from you!

www.ingramcontent.com/pod-product-compliance
Lightning Source LLC
Chambersburg PA
CBHW060509090426
42735CB00011B/2153